PROFESSIONAL POLICE-HUMAN RELATIONS TRAINING

(Second Printing)

Professional Police-Human Relations Training

ARTHUR I. SIEGEL
PHILIP J. FEDERMAN
DOUGLAS G. SCHULTZ

Applied Psychological Services
Wayne, Pennsylvania

With a Foreword by
ALBERT N. BROWN
Commissioner of Police
City of Philadelphia

CHARLES C THOMAS • PUBLISHER
Springfield • Illinois • U.S.A.

Published and Distributed Throughout the World by

CHARLES C THOMAS • PUBLISHER

BANNERSTONE HOUSE

301-327 East Lawrence Avenue, Springfield, Illinois, U.S.A.

© *1963, by* CHARLES C THOMAS   PUBLISHER

Library of Congress Catalog Card Number: 62-17613

First Printing, 1963
Second Printing, 1970

With THOMAS BOOKS careful attention is given to all details of manufacturing and design. It is the Publisher's desire to present books that are satisfactory as to their physical qualities and artistic possibilities and appropriate for their particular use. THOMAS BOOKS will be true to those laws of quality that assure a good name and good will.

Printed in the United States of America

2-00

To

Estelle
Beverly Lane
Margaret Claire

FOREWORD

THE PROFESSION OF LAW enforcement, even though young in the history of the honored professions, is rich in tradition because of its many heroic and meritorious services to the public whom it serves.

The law is a set of rules that are meant to regulate and guide the conduct of men by protecting the rights of the weak and the law-abiding from the aggressive acts of the evil-doers.

The policeman has been selected by the members of society to protect them against lawlessness with a minimum of disturbance and inconvenience. The role of the policeman in the community has changed greatly since the time he walked the streets through the night calling out the hour and that all was well. Today, his role in the community is far greater. He not only must be alert to preserve and protect the citizens under his care, but he must be able to comfort, guide and counsel those who are on the edge of or are involved in difficult situations. In order to do that competently, he must be able to understand the wants and needs of those who many times may be less fortunate than ourselves. We also have the duty to see that the rights of an offender, as guaranteed by the Constitution, are not in any way minimized or impaired.

The police officer of today is expected to handle an astonishing range of human problems and situations. He must approach these problems with a professional attitude, a high degree of skill, and impersonal objectivity. Realizing this, the Police Department engaged an outside firm to make a study of the relationship between the community and the police with the intention of preparing a course of instruction in human relations that would help the policeman to better understand people and thereby make him more competent to perform his daily tasks. To assure the success of the presentation of the course, a professional instructor was engaged to aid and assist the training division of the Philadelphia Police Department.

The profession of law enforcement, like all professions, must undergo constant study so that its skills, techniques, and knowledge keep pace with society's progress. This, in turn, improves the professional status of every policeman. The Police Command looks upon this training program as a worthwhile and essential step towards the professional growth of each member of the Philadelphia police force. To the trainees we address our hope that you will find the course interesting and helpful in your work. To those who do the training, we address our confidence that you will devote all the effort, skill and ingenuity at your command so that every class will add to the stature of the police force.

ALBERT N. BROWN
Commissioner of Police
City of Philadelphia

PREFACE

THESE CONFERENCE LEADER's materials for professional police-human relations training were originally prepared by Applied Psychological Services in consultation with the Commission on Human Relations, City of Philadelphia, for the Philadelphia Police Department.

In the autumn of 1957, the City of Philadelphia, in response to a felt need, decided to give its police officers additional training in the human relations aspects of their work. While human relations training had been previously given to police officers, its intensity was not sufficient. Accordingly a committee representing a number of knowledgeable community organizations was brought together to devise and develop a human relations training program to be integrated into the general training of all police officers. The committee recommended that persons proficient in human relations and in training be commissioned to prepare the necessary training materials. After a national search, Applied Psychological Services was given the appointment.

The first year of the effort was devoted to research in order to develop the background information required for such a course. This research involved a complete job analysis, derivation of performance requirements, formulation of training objectives and the development of training requirements. In order to accomplish these phases 75 Philadelphia police officers were interviewed in depth and police behavior was observed and recorded during 267 incidents.

The present volume represents the results of the second year's effort. This volume consists of a complete instructional package which can form the basis for a professional police-human relations training course. Section I consists of an instructor's or conference leader's manual. Section II contains the required case materials. Section III contains lecture outlines. These lectures are to be given at the conclusion of each discussion.

The course itself is based on the case method of presentation. It is felt that the case method, with its free, informal atmosphere, provides the best vehicle for success, with the type of indoctrinational material involved. The cases included all were written to meet the criteria of:

(1) *Realism*—to increase motivation and to reinforce positive cues.

(2) *Completeness*—to decrease speculative thinking.

(3) *Problem inclusion*—to take advantage of the learn-by-doing concept.

(4) *Thought provocation*—to allow for entrance into the discussion of officers with different points of view and to allow for intensive investigation of various solution avenues.

(5) *Decision demanding*—to allow "closure."

(6) *Currentness*—to provide a basis for "transfer of training" to similar situations which the student will meet on his duty assignment.

In the initial trial of these materials, each class was headed by two conference leaders: (1) a police officer, and (2) a qualified social scientist. It was considered most appropriate that police officer training of this type be given primarily by fellow officers. However, since technical questions involving the social sciences were almost certain to arise in each meeting, the social science resource person was considered to be a required supplement. Additionally, the social scientist was responsible for delivering the lectures. The results indicated success beyond original hopes and expectations.

It is believed that this work represents a long step beyond the "good will" school of human relations training. The material allows the student the opportunity to analyze in depth many of the factors involved in ordinary police work which can produce either positive or negative human relations responses.

Human relations training for police officers is merely one step in the professionalization of a police force. It is not new.

Ever since the race riots which occurred in East St. Louis, Chicago, and Washington during and after World War I, various Governor's Commissions, Mayor's Committees and civic councils have made recommendations for police-human relations training. In 1942, Dr. Gordon Allport of Harvard University published a report on an experiment in this type of training and Joseph Kluchesky wrote a report on the subject in 1946. Similarly, Dr. Joseph Lohman developed a course which was used by the Southern Police Institute. In more recent years the National Conference of Christians and Jews has promoted such programs and Michigan State University has conducted a number of institutes on this type of training. The police academies in Detroit, Philadelphia, and Los Angeles, are said to include some training in intergroup relations as part of the recruit training.

Complete, comprehensive, thorough training of both recruits and in-service police personnel is but one factor in the professionalization of a police force. Other considerations include, but are not limited to:

(1) Clearly defined, fairly administered codes of behavior and standards of performance.

(2) High selection standards from both the mental capacity and personal adjustment points of view.

(3) A salary scale suitable for attracting and holding qualified personnel.

(4) An intelligent top command which is free from political pressures.

(5) Application of modern personnel management methods including proper performance evaluation and review, and clearly defined lines of advancement involving career planning.

(6) A community relations program designed to encourage police-citizen cooperation and public readiness to support and cooperate with the police.

(7) Appropriation adequate for continued requisite in-service training, adequate equipment, and facilities.

(8) A working relationship with and professional recognition by other municipal agencies.

Human relations training, like any other training, will be most effective if it is periodically reinforced. This reinforcement can come from a program of posters, leaflets, statements at musters, and communications from the top command. Additionally, a system of reward for extraordinary action in the human relations aspects of police work and the incorporation of these rewards in the performance record of the officer will be helpful.

It is pointed out that the material here included is "introductory" and "basic." Advanced and special courses for higher echelon officers and special units may still be needed, but would have to be especially planned.

We would like to express our indebtedness to the others who have contributed to this work. Albert Brown, Commissioner of Police, City of Philadelphia, contributed the full cooperation and resources at his command in support of the work. Similarly, Deputy Commissioner of Police Howard Leary provided needed information, liaison, and facilitation from several points of view. Harry Fox, former Superintendent, Philadelphia Police Academy, contributed materially to our understanding of police training problems. George Schermer, Executive Director, Commission on Human Relations, City of Philadelphia, and Burton Gordin, Deputy Director of the City's Commission on Human Relations, provided advice, encouragement, and technical opinion throughout the work. We are especially indebted to the Technical Advisory Committee on Human Relations Training for Police Personnel in Philadelphia for their guidance and for their several contributions. The members of this committee include: Christopher F. Edley, Charles P. Cella, Jr., Martin P. Chworowsky, Samuel Dash, Nathan L. Edelstein, Maurice B. Fagan, William N. Gillin, Thomas M. Reed, Ira A. Reid, Stephen B. Sweeney, Milton H. Washington.

The materials contained herein have been used initially in Philadelphia. However, the application of these materials demands police officers to serve as conference leaders who have been selected in accordance with the special requirements of the course, specially selected resource support personnel, and general training and specific indoctrination in the use of the materials for both. Accordingly, these materials should not be used for training purposes unless these conditions have been met. Permission is granted for reproduction of the "group material" in Section II, when it is to be used for police instructional purposes.

ARTHUR I. SIEGEL
PHILIP J. FEDERMAN
DOUGLAS G. SCHULTZ

CONTENTS

SECTION I

CONFERENCE LEADER'S MANUAL

[xv]

SECTION II

CASE AND ROLE PLAYING MATERIALS

Contents

SECTION III

LECTURE MATERIALS

PROFESSIONAL POLICE-HUMAN RELATIONS TRAINING

SECTION I
CONFERENCE LEADER'S MANUAL

CHAPTER 1

WHAT THESE MATERIALS CONTAIN

TRAINING POLICE OFFICERS in the human relations aspects of their work has proven valuable in a number of cities. New York, Detroit, and Los Angeles are examples of cities which have incorporated human relations study into their police training programs. In Philadelphia, the top police officials, in consultation with the Commission on Human Relations of the City and a large number of civic organizations, gave careful consideration to the usefulness of such a program. They decided that additional training in the human relations aspects of police officer work would be a major practical benefit to all police officers in the conduct of their daily duties. As a result of that decision, the best talent available was brought together to study the problem and prepare the necessary training materials. These materials represent the results. The manual contains three sections. Section I is a manual of instructions for the police officer trainers. Section II contains the required training or case materials. Section III incorporates lecture material. These lectures are to be presented by a resource person(s) who assist(s) in all class meetings.

What is the Case Method?

Experience has indicated that lecturing to a class is not the best method for teaching the type of material involved in the human relations aspects of police officer work. It has also been shown that an instructional method known as the case method can produce the desired results.

In the case method, a real life episode is presented. What each person involved in the episode did and said is given along with appropriate background information. Then a group discussion of the episode or case is held under the guidance of the conference leader. Each person in the group tells how he feels about the various acts and decisions of the people involved in the episode. Because of the nature of the cases, real differences of opinion emerge in the discussion. The exploration of these differences and their causes constitute an important step in the alteration of attitudes.

It has been said that education does not consist of teaching people to know what they do not know; it means teaching them to behave as they do not behave. To generalize to our context, we are not interested in giving police officers human relations knowledge *per se,* but are interested in modifying their behavior from the professional police-human relations points of view. We are interested in *training* police officers in the human relations aspects of their work, not in educating them as social scientists.

The behaviors which we are interested in changing are those which can be ascribed to faulty attitudes and opinions. A frontal lecture, or "father knows best" attack on attitude and opinion change is probably bound to fail. Such an attempt will, without question, merely evoke hositility and a set of reasons justifying already held feelings, as well as deeper self-justification. It should be possible to modify individual police officer attitudes if: (1) the range of the experience of the individual police officers can be broadened; (2) it can be shown that certain practices fail to satisfy the needs of the police department; (3) the notions and opinions of the individual police officer can be altered; (4) it can be shown to the police officer that attitudinal change will not result in shutting him out from his friends and co-workers, and (5) it can be shown to the police officer that attitudinal change will improve his skills, his chances for advancement, and public attitudes towards the force.

Little or no progress can be made toward revising a police officer's attitudes unless he can be made uncertain about some of his current attitudes and how they may not square with the needs of the police department. The case method, with its free, informal atmosphere and divergent opinions constitutes an ideal medium for raising doubt in the police officer's mind about his current attitudes. If it can be shown to the police officer that his actions, as dictated by his attitudes, notions and points of view fail to help him to act effectively, attitudinal change may be achieved.

A new attitude, if it is to be accepted, must be developed together with a person's social and work group. If possible, a police officer group must take part in creating the new attitude. The case method permits this collaborative interaction.

Moreover, as a police officer's attitudes change in the group situation, the change is seen as accepted by the group (non-ostracism) and as one which came from the group. Thus, the change is more freely accepted.

Furthermore, it has been amply shown that a prime factor in learning is motivation. One motivating force in police officer training is the usefulness of the course material to the on-the-job requirements as the police officer sees them. Therefore, any course must be presented in a manner that makes its applicability clear. The case method is an ideal vehicle for achieving this purpose.

Role Playing

Role playing represents a case technique that simulates real life more closely. In role playing, the individuals act out parts. However, there is no script. The individual remains himself and lets his ideas and attitudes become modified as the situation evolves. Moreover, in role playing, the student receives the opportunity to practice, and to "feel" the emotions and thinking of people who may be different from him. This opportunity may not be available in case discussion.

Moreover, some attitudinal modification depends on the individual development of a clear understanding of the motives and actions of others. Role playing meets these conditions and has been used in a variety of educational procedures including industrial training and community leader training. One area in which role playing has been successful has been the development of industrial supervisors from line workers. When a worker moves to the foreman level, a new orientation towards bosses and buddies is often required. Consequently, attitudinal reorientation is an important aspect of foreman training.

During the session several people may act out the "hot role."

At the close of the session, the group discusses the behaviors of the participants and asks them to analyze critically their own behavior. In this manner, insights into his attitudes and interpersonal relationships are developed by the police officer.

Outcomes of This Training

There are several outcomes from this type of training. First, the police officer's attitudes towards his job needs and job requirements are modified along desirable avenues. Second, skill in dealing with police-human relations problems of a practical everyday nature is developed. Third, needed knowledges are incidentally acquired in a police-human relations context. Fourth, human relations thinking habits that are realistic and objective are developed. Fifth, preconceptions are replaced with understanding.

Why it Will Work for Your Groups

Experience in a large number of industrial organizations has demonstrated that the case method works. The same principles that are followed in developing industrial case material have been followed in preparing the material in Section II of this manual.

These case materials are not ivy tower or academic stuff which does not apply to realistic police officers. They are based on an analysis of actual incidents which occurred in Philadelphia. An extensive study was made to insure their practicality and reality. As a result, you will find that officers are able to identify easily with the materials. They will respond energetically to each case. In your conference leader's role, you will lead a discussion about each case. As you lead the discussion, the officers will react to your leads and in so doing they will start to make progress towards increased proficiency in the human relations aspects of a police officer's work.

You can see that the case method is based largely on the "learn-by-doing" concept. Ideas and experience become connected. Moreover, by allowing the total group to participate, advantage is taken of the pooled effect of the group's experience and skill. Thus, anyone who can benefit from experience will profit from the course, and we can expect positive results with police officers.

Why You are Qualified as a Conference Leader

You are qualified as a conference leader first and foremost because of your years of experience as a police officer. As a result, you know police work. Additionally, you know the police organization in which you work—procedures, policies, methods, resources, and chain-of-command.

Second, you know police officers and how they think, feel, and react. This knowledge will allow you to lead skillfully the discussion with a sensitivity and awareness which no outsider could bring to the task.

Admittedly, not every experienced police officer could act as a conference leader in this course. A special set of qualifications is needed. These qualifications include energy, brains and verbal power, plus the ability to: (1) size up situations; (2) work on a team; (3) make decisions, and (4) get along with people. You were selected, out of a large number of candidates, because you possess these attributes.

However, there are two additional ingredients needed for doing the kind of conference leadership job you are capable of doing. The first of these is experience in leading group discussions. We overcome this deficiency in two ways. The first part of this manual provides some necessary background information. This material will be supplemented by a series of meetings with the people who wrote this manual or with other qualified case method resource persons. They will try to answer your questions and to offer additional hints. You will also conduct a number of practice meetings under the guidance of these experienced leaders. At the end of each of these meetings a detailed briefing will be held with you to help you sharpen your skills. Thus, you can be sure that you are well prepared, even for your first course presentation.

The second additional ingredient required is formal training in the social sciences. But you don't have to hit the books and cram in a lot of academic theory before you can start. Capable social resource personnel will be appointed to help you in each class meeting. While you are principally responsible for carrying the ball, he will be able to answer theoretical questions and questions of fact which involve a knowledge of the social scientific disciplines.

Will the Case Method be Entirely Relied On?

In each meeting, the social scientist will also present a thirty minute talk. This talk will contain information about certain matters which might not ordinarily be brought out through case discussions. The outline for each of these lectures is presented in the third section of this manual. Topics such as *Individual and Group Similarities and Differences* and *Community Human Relations Resources* are included in these lectures.

Where Did the Cases Come From?

We have said that the case materials which you will use are realistic and practical. How do we know this? We know this because of an extensive study* of the operational human relations performance requirements for police officers. In this study, a large number of Philadelphia's police officers were interviewed and observations were made over a representative sample of districts. In addition, a number of knowledgeable community human relations officials were interviewed extensively. As a result of the information so developed, ten incident types were chosen as representing the most critical and frequently met operational human relations aspects of police officer work. These incident types were:

(1) Argumentative married couple
(2) Argumentative neighbors
(3) Burglary investigation
(4) Car stop
(5) Crowd
(6) Drunk
(7) Fights and riots
(8) House search
(9) Molested female
(10) Street lounging

---

* Siegel, A. I., and Baker, R. C.: *Police-human Relations Training.* Prepared by Applied Psychological Services, Wayne, Pa., for the Police Department and Commission on Human Relations, City of Philadelphia.

It is these incident types which will form the basis for your class meetings.

How the Cases are Organized

The studies that were carried out indicated that most police incidents can be examined sequentially by stages. These stages, which may occur at any place, (on the street, in the patrol wagon, in the police station, in court, etc.) are:

Initial entry—	Those police activities which take place between the time the police officer arrives on the scene and the time that he starts to obtain the facts of an incident through questioning or other methods.
Fact finding—	Those police activities which involve the development of the necessary information for deciding upon a course of action.
Data evaluation—	The process of appropriately considering all the facts available prior to deciding upon an appropriate course of action.
Decision making—	The actual formulation of a specific course of action to pursue in order to resolve an incident.
Consummating the plan—	Those activities between the actual decision on a specific course of action to pursue and the time at which the police officer no longer has contact with the parties concerned.

Each of these stages involves specific police officer human relations attitudes, knowledges, skills and decisions.

The incorporation of each of the stages into each case along with the required police officer-human relations attitudes, knowledges, and skills can be presented as a three dimensional model as shown in Figure 1. Such a model is helpful in clearly defining and visualizing the total goals to be obtained by the use of the case materials. In Figure 1, the total cube represents the composite of the case training materials. The rows represent each incident type and the columns represent the human relations attitudes, knowledges, skills and decisions represented in each stage. These content materials are also represented by the lines in each

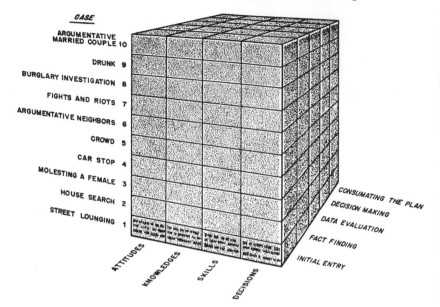

Figure 1. Schematic representation of units in course.

cube and which, in a sense, fill the cube. The slices represent the stages of the issues and subissues in each case. These are organized into the initial entry, fact finding, data evaluation, etc., stages. The model when filled represents the entire course. However, each individual cube may be presented as a short specific unit.

Each of the cases included in Section II of this manual is broken into a unit which represents one of the cubes in the model. However, not all cubes are included for each case. This is because the attitudes, knowledges, and skills represented by an omitted cube are covered in another part of the course.

Let's Get Down to Cases

By now you have probably said to yourself, "These are nice generalities but what do I have to do exactly?" A conference leader in the case discussion has the responsibility for leading (not running) the discussion. Thus, your role is that of an expediter. After the necessary background material for an individual stage has been distributed, the class is divided into groups of about ten persons. You will have about twenty persons in the class and thus will be able to form two groups. You also appoint a leader for each group. Each group is allowed ten minutes to prepare arguments on a question relevant to the case. After ten minutes, you reconvene the class and the leader of one group presents the opinions of his group. After the leader has given his group's position, the position is opened to discussion by all members of the class.

Following this discussion, the leader of the second group presents his group's position and another discussion takes place.

This procedure is then repeated for the other incident stages.

During the discussion, your job is to provide a permissive atmosphere—one in which each person feels that he has a right to express his own opinion. In a very real sense, your success as a discussion leader can be measured by how little you speak and by how much each and every group member speaks.

However, you must conduct more than a "gab festival." There is a certain amount of progress or a given number of points which should be considered in the discussion of each incident stage. It is your job to keep the discussion on the track. Chapter 2 of this manual contains a number of hints for accomplishing this. It is also your job to ensure that the discussion includes as many as possible of the issues presented under the heading "Discussion Points" which is included with each case stage. You can make sure that these points are included by asking leading questions such as: "How do you feel about ————? Do you think it is important that ————? Would it ever happen that ————? Do you think that ————? Have you ever thought that ————? Let's consider ————?"

Thus, while encouraging a free atmosphere, you will have to guide the discussion to a series of conclusions. Moreover, and of primary importance, at the end of the discussion of each incident stage, it is necessary for you to summarize the conclusions reached in the discussion of the arguments of each group. While your role during the discussion is generally retiring, your role in the summary is to reflect a point of view. This point of view is generally implicit in the "Discussion Points" section included with each case and explicit in the objectives of the course.

Training Objectives

The extent to which your course will be successful depends upon your ability to make it meet the training objectives. These training objectives were derived after a thorough study of the expectations of the police officer held by police officials, community officials, and the public at large.

Training Objective 1—The Development in Police Officers of an Appreciation of the Civil Rights of the Public

One of the most fundamental elements in any police course in human relations is civil rights. This statement is applicable to police dealings with any and every citizen. It is imperative for all police officers to appreciate the civil rights acknowledged to the public by law.

Research data strongly support the need for such course content in any police-human relations training program. For instance, it has been found that many police officers tend to be overly forceful when dealing with citizens who are ignorant of their civil rights. False arrests, illegal entries, and general denial of the civil liberties of the public are condemned as professional police practice.

Training Objective 2—The Development in Police Officers of the Ability to Meet Without Undue Militance, Aggressiveness, Hostility, or Prejudice, Police Situations Involving Minority Groups

Closely akin to an appreciation of the civil rights of the public is the ability of the police officer to refrain from any unnecessary hostility or militance when dealing with minority group members.

Knowledgeable community officials have maintained that police officers often tend to act in an unreasonably aggressive manner to some segments of the population. In general, they feel that the police officer should learn to use force prudently, and only as a last resort. Public opinion survey comparisons between white and Negro citizens also strongly document the need for incorporating Training Objective 2 into a training program in the human relations aspects of police officer work. The police officer should gain an awareness of the need to treat people of all races and religions with equal fairness and to use force wisely.

Training Objective 3—The Development in Police Officers of an Adequate Social Perspective

This training objective is actually a corollary to Training Objective 2 and its aim is to develop within the police officer, when he deals with people on his job, an adequate democratic outlook. When dealing with minority group members, this outlook is an especially important requisite. In order to accomplish this goal, it is necessary for the officer to gain an understanding of the attitudes, "cultures," and idiosyncrasies of various segments of the population.

This objective involves the development of such behaviors and understandings:

(a) Being courteous and respectful.
(b) Refraining from name calling and the use of epithets.
(c) Avoiding insults and humiliating citizens.
(d) Serving, guiding and helping others.
(e) Understanding the problems that many minority group members encounter.
(f) Understanding the unique "cultures" of minority groups for a better understanding of their motives, desires, and overt behaviors.

Training Objective 4—The Development in Police Officers of an Awareness of Individual and Group Differences

An important contributing factor to the police officer's social perspective is an awareness of individual and group differences. If the police officer is to be polite and understanding when dealing with minority group members, he must first be taught to avoid the pitfall of broad overgeneralization. This means that he must become cognizant of the fact that, for example, even if he knows a criminal with dark skin, the majority of dark-skinned people are not criminals. There is a need, then, for the police officer to differentiate among individuals as personalities apart from their race, religion, or national origin.

Thus, the police officer must learn to make distinctions among members of a minority group (i.e., all Negroes are not criminals), and to deal objectively with a given incident rather than become side-tracked because of the race, religion, or national origin of the parties concerned.

Training Objective 5—The Development of an Understanding by Police Officers of How Their Words and Actions May Be Perceived by the Public

One critical psychological aspect to the practice of good human relations procedures is the ability to understand how one's spoken and physical behaviors will be seen and interpreted by others. It is often the case that people tend to behave without any thought of the results of their actions. These people actually think and act in a social vacuum; the result of their actions is confusion, irritation, hostility, and ill-will between the parties concerned.

The importance of Training Objective 5 was brought out in the research behind this manual in which it was found that many police officers do not have an understanding of the public's problems because of their inability to place themselves emotionally in the shoes of the public. Consequently, the public is perceived as just "numbers" rather than as a group of unique personalities who warrant careful consideration and deep thought before any action is taken.

As a result of the police officer's lack of ability to place himself in the role of the average citizen, he will often manifest such undesirable behaviors as impoliteness, abuse of personal property, undue militance, and lack of objectivity when confronting community members. Therefore, one of the results of the police-human relations training program must be the development of an understanding in police officers of how their words and actions may be interpreted by the public.

Training Objective 6—The Development in Police Officers of an Acceptance of Integrated Situations

One of the major social trends during the past few decades has been an increase in racial integration in employment, housing, and in the schools. Since integration is a real phenomenon that will probably gain momentum in the future and because it is closely related to the problem of human relations, one of the objectives of the police-human relations course is the development of an acceptance of integrated situations. By the word "acceptance" we focus primarily upon "acceptable police behavior" and secondarily upon "acceptable police attitudes." Since integration is a social phenomenon, only peripherally related to the police officer's on-the-job responsibilities, it is thought not necessary to focus considerable course energy on altering attitudes on this issue. In other words, the police officer should be (and in fact is) allowed to choose the location of his home, the particular school that his children attend, and with whom he wishes to associate socially. However, because of the special demands of his police position, his on-the-job actions should in no way conflict with the legal or social aspects of integration.

Training Objective 7—To Develop in Police Officers a Knowledge of the Fact that Their Behavior Will Infuse Similar Inter-group Behaviors and Attitudes in Other Members of the Police Force

One of the most frequently expressed opinions during interviews with members of the police force was that what is learned about police work is learned primarily from on-the-job experience. Logically, then, a trainee must look towards the more experienced members of the police force for guidance and knowledge. As a result, the youthful trainee tends to incorporate within himself those police "attitudes," "skills," and "knowledges" manifested by his superiors and more experienced peers. Under these circumstances, the situation is ripe for spreading either desirable or undesirable human relations attitudes and practices. In fact, the success of any human relations course will depend, in large, upon the attitudes and practices of older members of the force with whom the recent graduate comes in contact. This means that both established police personnel and the new recruit must learn that their behavior will create similar intergroup behaviors and attitudes in other members of the police force.

Training Objective 8—The Development in Police Officers of a Recognition and Awareness of the Role of Associated Community Human Relations Agencies

In order to emphasize how associated community agencies can help the police officer with problems of a human relations nature, it is important that the training includes an indoctrination in the role of associated community agencies. To be utterly frank, research has indicated that many police officers are of the opinion that community human relations agencies are composed of professional and political "do-gooders" whose primary purpose in life is to publicize and to exaggerate alleged police misconduct. As a result of the course, the officer should gain a recognition and awareness of the goals of these agencies and to accept and use these agencies as an aid in achieving harmonious police-public inter-group relations.

Training Objective 9—The Development in Police Officers of the Skills Requisite for Anticipating and Meeting the Police-Human Relations Aspects of: (a) Their Work, (b) Incidents Rooted in Factors of Race, Religion, and National Origin, (c) Juvenile Offenses, (d) Civil Rights Complaints, and (e) Community Tensions

A composite of the explicit and implicit aspects of the preceding eight training objectives would result in Training Objective 9. Although this objective represents an overall and summary type of objective, it further clarifies the principal results to be gained from the course in the human relations aspects of police officer work.

The Procedure in Action

Now that we have provided you with some necessary background information, let's see how you will actually use the training materials. Section II of this manual contains all the materials needed for each meeting. Moreover, the materials are divided into the appropriate stage units to be considered for each case: initial entry, fact finding, data evaluation, etc. Where material in Section II is marked "Group Material" additional copies of this material should be duplicated for distribution to the group members. Consider Case I of Section II, "Street Lounging." The first material is marked "Stage 1"—"Initial Entry"—"Group

---

Group Material

CASE I—STREET LOUNGING
STAGE 1—INITIAL ENTRY

On a hot, humid summer night, at 12:30 a.m., Officers Johnson and Romanowicz, while on squad car patrol, observed a crowd of seven to eight men on a corner across the street from the Silver Dollar Bar and Grill. The neighborhood in which the bar is located is composed of low income families who live in small, six-room row houses. Many are privately owned; others are rented at nominal rates. Since the congregants seemed to be loud and boisterous, the police officers stopped their car near the crowd of men. The men, in their late twenties to early thirties, seemed to be casually clothed; they wore lightweight cotton trousers and tee shirts. One man stood out in the crowd. He seemed somewhat older than the others and was wearing a light tropical suit, a white shirt buttoned at the collar, a tie, and a panama hat.

Officer Romanowicz leaned out of the car window and asked the group not to congregate on the street. Although none of the residents in the neighborhood had complained to the police, Officer Romanowicz further stated that the police had received a complaint.

The men did not say anything to the officers. However, they displayed their annoyance and belligerence toward the officer's request in the manner in which they walked away and by the expressions on their faces.

Exhibit 1. Group material for Case I, Stage 1.

Group A: Some experts maintain that certain environmental factors lead to behavior such as street lounging. What
might these be and what other reasons can you offer
for explaining why people may congregate on streets?
Given the same environmental factors, would all people
act the same? Is it within the rights of citizens to congregate on street corners? Why are street loungers often
reluctant to disperse?

Group B: Were Officers Johnson and Romanowicz within their
rights when they asked the group to disperse? Justify
your answer. Would you, in a similar situation, explain
the reason for your request to the street loungers? Was
it proper for Officer Romanowicz to tell the street
loungers that one of the nearby residents had complained? What are the possible consequences of such
a lie?

Exhibit 2. Huddle questions for "Street Lounging"—"Initial Entry."

Material." These labels tell you the stage of the incident and that
this is handout material.

Accordingly, you distribute the *duplicated* handout to the
students. A copy of this handout is also shown as Exhibit 1.

After you distribute the handout material, you divide your
class into two groups and appoint a chairman for each group. The
members of each group are then given copies of their group's
question. You will have white and Negro officers in your class
and each group should be composed of members of each race.
The groups will be given ten minutes to prepare arguments on
their assigned question(s). The questions are located directly
below the case material. A sufficient number of these huddle
questions will have to be prepared as separates for distribution
to the groups. Exhibit 2 is a reproduction of the assignments
for the initial entry stage of the street lounging case. Once the
groups have received their assignments they huddle and prepare
arguments on their assigned questions.

After ten minute huddles, the whole group reassembles and
now you are ready for the discussion. It may be helpful at this

point to write the huddle questions on the blackboard so that each group can see the other group's question(s) during the discussion.

The Discussion

The spokesman for the first committee is given approximately one minute to state the point(s) of view of the members of the committee he represents. Then the point(s) of view are opened to the class for rebuttal, criticism, and elaboration. Allow ten minutes for this discussion; everyone should take part. Following this discussion, present your summary and then repeat the process starting with the spokesman for the second committee. After you have summarized for the second committee, the total process is repeated for the next presented stage of the case, and then for the third presented stage.

Certain human relations aspects of police work should be considered during these discussions. These "Discussion Points" for each stage are listed in Section II on the last page of each stage. It may happen that these points emerge from the discussion naturally. If so, all well and good. If the points do not emerge, you will have to inject as many of them as possible into the discussion through leading questions. The discussion points for the initial entry stage of the street lounging case are shown in Exhibit 3.

Budgeting Time

Each meeting will consume three hours. If you allow thirty minutes to each of the three presented aspects of each case, the huddles and discussion periods will fill ninety minutes. The lecture material and lecture discussion should consume no more than sixty minutes. The remaining thirty minutes of the three hour period will be filled by your summaries and two smoke breaks of ten minutes each.

However, play the exact allocation of time by ear. You may find that the discussion is progressing well, that you are having little difficulty in bringing out the required discussion points, and that it does not seem possible to drop a discussion when the clock runs out. If this occurs, do not feel obliged to stop the

Attitudes	Knowledges	Skills
How a person's "present mood" determines how he will react to other people	Why street corner loungers may be reluctant to disperse	Asking a group of street corner loungers to disperse
	Why some people feel abused or "picked on" by the police	Dispersing a group of street corner loungers
	Why some people possess an arrogant attitude toward the police	Explaining the law to people
	The ways in which certain people think	Making quick decisions on a course of action to follow
	The sense of values that people possess	Taking action that you think your supervisors would want you to take
	Ethics and professionalism in police work	
	The civil rights laws	

Exhibit 3. Discussion points for "Street Lounging"—"Initial Entry."

discussion. Allow it to continue as long as you feel that you are making progress. This may mean that you do not cover all the stages provided for each case. This is all right provided that continual progress is made towards the course's objectives.

Remember, the case materials are only a mechanism for getting into the discussion. They are not an end but a means toward an end.

Suppose the Discussion Runs Out of Steam

Due to the nature of the case materials, you will have little trouble keeping the discussion on the track. However, the discussion could run into a road block and bog down. Especially at the outset, possibly as a hold-over from previous school training, some of the members may assume that a few people should do all the talking and the rest should go along with the game. Or, they may not want to talk because they are afraid of pulling a "boner." Others may have the attitude that you can make them

---

1. How could popular magazines and newspapers have contributed to the attitude shown toward the police by the loungers?

2. Do you think that street loungers view themselves as violators of the law?

3. Could personality mechanisms such as repressed tensions and frustrations be expressing themselves in the behaviors of the loungers?

4. How does frustration manifest itself in such behaviors as: (a) crime and radicalism, (b) aggression against authority, (c) self punishment, (d) group identification?

5. Could the dress of the loungers be interpreted as a prestige symbol similar to the yacht of the businessman or the political leanings of some college students? How so?

6. Should police officers explain to street loungers why they are asking them to disperse? Why?

Exhibit 4. Lead questions for "Street Lounging"—"Initial Entry."

show up for a discussion but that you can't force them to participate or that talk is cheap and that this is nothing but talk.

A series of lead questions is also provided with each case stage. You may direct these or similar questions to the reluctant members or to the group in order to stimulate discussion. The lead questions for the initial entry stage of the street lounging incident are shown in Exhibit 4.

CHAPTER 2

GETTING STARTED, DIGGING IN, AND REACHING THE OBJECTIVES

It is best if you make up your classes of either: (1) patrolmen and sergeants, or (2) captains and lieutenants.

Both you and your group members may be nervous at the start of the first meeting. This is natural and possibly to be expected. You will only know some of the members and possibly only a few will know you. Moreover, this will be a new experience for the group members who will be accustomed to more formal methods of instruction and whose thinking may not be entirely in harmony with objectives of the course.

Thus, a degree of flexibility will be needed in the first meeting. To a large extent, the success of the total course will depend on how well you get started.

Beginning the First Meeting

You should spend not more than twenty to thirty minutes at the beginning of the first meeting explaining the why and how of the course and introducing the class members to each other. Your remarks should be as brief as possible but should set the tone for the following classes. Try to give the strong impression that this will not be a formal lecture course and that participation by everyone is welcome and expected.

Some typical opening remarks are given below. But you can make these points however you wish. The important point is not the precise wording but that *all* the points are covered. For this reason, it may be helpful if you make an outline on a card or paper listing the major headings below and jotting down a few notes under each heading to remind you of what should be mentioned.

Introductions

The first thing to do is to introduce yourself and the social scientist; then ask each class member to give his name and perhaps the district where he is assigned. You might say something like the following:

"You are working members of the police force and so am I. And we are here to work. We are going to work at police work and at improving our effectiveness. My name is —————. Dr. ————— will also take part in these discussions and present a short talk on a topic related to the course during the final hour of each meeting. Since we are going to meet for ten meetings, we might as well know each other's names."

At this point, ask each member to introduce himself.

Attendance

You should stress the importance of attendance at every meeting. Something like: "In order to benefit from this course you must be present. There is no text that you can read afterwards. Attendance is required and we are going to have roll call."

Nature and Purpose of Course

Try to point out that: (1) the course employs the case method, (2) the cases are taken from actual police work, and (3) as a result of this, the officer can expect to become more effective on the job.

"We are going to be discussing the human relations aspects of the work of the police officer. The way these meetings are going to be held is called the case method. In the case method, a real incident is described. Then each of us will tell each other what we think about the incident, how we think it could have been handled better, what we think was done wrông or right, and why the officers and citizens involved might have acted as they did. Through this, we hope to develop the kind of on-the-street behavior that will improve your skills, your chances for promotion, and public attitudes toward the force. We will get some new ideas or new angles about professional police work. Instead of one point of view, we will pick up each other's points of view. And in so doing, we will automatically be developing our skills."

Class Members' Responsibilities

It should be made clear that the classes will be mostly discussion of the cases. The real purpose of the meetings is to give everyone a chance to express his point of view, the reasons for it, and to listen to others. It is each class member's responsibility to speak, listen, and think. There are no "right" answers, tests, or marks.

You might make the following kinds of comments: "We will have two kinds of work here. First, everyone is expected to contribute to the discussion. Whether you agree or disagree your reasons are important. There is no censorship of ideas, no tests or marks, and probably no one has all the answers. Few are all right or all wrong. Everyone has the right to his own opinion and his opinion is wanted and will be respected—no matter how popular or unpopular it may be. Your second job here is that of a listener. Each person should listen to and try to understand the other fellow's point of view. How to listen is something many people, including my wife, haven't learned. Only by listening to someone can we learn what he is thinking. While we listen, we should think about how the other fellow's remarks might have helped us in some of our work. In this way, we'll be putting together a body of ideas—and since talk can't get far, so long as it is just talk, you should try some of the ideas on the job.

You might also observe the other members as they talk. Notice that some think with their feelings instead of their heads. If you can spot this in others, also try spotting it in yourself. If you spot it in yourself, look inside yourself and ask if it also happens on the job—and if so, why?

In this way, we will start to understand ourselves and others and why people may act and say what they do in various situations. We will start to see how our attitudes, biases, prejudices, and early experiences and those of other people affect day-to-day behavior in subtle ways. Once we recognize these, we will be starting to know something about what other people are thinking and feeling. This will be of major practical benefit on the street.

To a degree, most police actions can be thought of as actions involving social relationships and situations—ones involving the interaction of people. A social situation consists of the present and the future, things that *are* and of things which *become* what people make them. Moreover, they are constantly changing. We must be able to grasp quickly minor details, to view facts in their proper relationship, to appreciate social change, and to make statements in a social situation that are factual and objective but which do not emotionally stir up citizens. This will serve to make you a more effective police officer."

Background for Course

Here the class should learn a little of the extensive work that backs up the course and should be told the fact that other cities are doing very much the same kind of thing. Also, it should be mentioned that the course has topside support and that various other professions such as teachers, recreation workers, and religious leaders are receiving similar training. Perhaps the following:

"Now you may have already said to yourself, 'Go blow, this I need like a hole in the head.' Let me assure you that this training is not a quick snow job and it was not taken up lightly. Other cities such as Chicago, New York, St. Louis, and Los Angeles are also giving such subject matter to their police officers. The Commissioner originated the idea for this course and has been in on this since its inception. It has been in planning and development for two and one-half years. The course developers interviewed over 75 Philadelphia police officers and rode in squad cars for two months. You can see that this is not a will-o-the-wisp. Every police officer, including captains and lieutenants, in Philadelphia will eventually get this training. Moreover, similar training is being given to teachers, recreation workers, and religious leaders. As a result, their jobs have been made easier. We anticipate the same results here and that your work will be easier for you as a result.

"Now, if you have any questions to this point I'll be glad to answer them. (Take and answer any questions and then continue.) If that's all the questions, let me give you some of the details on how we will function."

The Way the Classes will be Run

The classroom mechanics should be discussed so the members know what to expect. The kinds of cases and the way they are organized should be described. The way the discussion groups will be formed and their function should be made clear. You might say something like:

"In each of the ten meetings we will be working on a specific case. These include: car stop, street lounging, fights and riots, burglary investigation, and so forth. Each case is organized by stages. The *initial entry* stage is composed of those activities which took place between the time the police officers involved in the case arrived on the scene and when they started to obtain the facts through questioning or other methods. The *fact finding* stage is composed of those police activities involved in the development of the necessary information for deciding upon a course of action. The *data evaluative* stage consists of appropriate consideration by the officers involved of all the facts available prior to deciding upon an appropriate course of action. The *decision making* stage consists of the actual development of a specific course of action to follow in order to close the case. The last stage, called *consummating the plan,* covers the time between the actual decision on a specific course of action to follow and when the officers involved no longer had contact with the parties concerned.

"However, because of time limitations, we will not discuss every stage in every case. Here is how it will work. I will distribute the necessary informational material. Then I will subdivide the class into two groups. Each group will have a leader. Each time a different person will be the leader and I will continually mix the groups. Each group will huddle and have ten minutes to prepare arguments on questions which I will give about the case. At the end of the ten minutes, we will reconvene and the leader will present the opinions and decisions of the group he represents. Then we will open these opinions and decisions to everyone for discussion, elaboration, and reconsideration.

"After we have discussed the opinions of the first group, we will allow the leader of the other team to present the feelings of his team on their question. Then we will repeat the discussion process for the question given the second team.

"Now are there any other questions; if not, let's try the first case."

Questions

Be sure everyone is clear about the purposes and procedures. Urge the class members to ask about anything they do not understand.

TIPS FOR PROGRESS

Once the class has reconvened your role as co-chairman involves leading the discussion and ensuring that the necessary discussion points are covered. You must be able to hold to the course objectives which may be unacceptable or only acceptable in theory to certain class members. However, you must not force these principles on persons who are not willing to accept them as yet.

The Climate

The climate you maintain should be democratic and permissive. In this climate, you must stimulate thinking without dominating the class. You must be sure that everyone gets heard. If the argument gets hung up because members are merely disagreeing over the meaning of words, you must clarify the word usage.

When dealing with the type of material involved, the discussion may occasionally get hot. No matter how heated the discussion, you should remain level-headed. Try to impersonalize the discussion. Avoid making anyone appear to be a fool or a bigot. List the facts on the board. Above all, allow the emotional person to speak his say. Then you might ask others if they are convinced by his arguments and why his arguments might be wrong.

Occasionally, you may be forced to shut off the discussion.

A good technique for doing this is to refer the issue to the class by a question such as, "Don't you think that we have pursued this as far as we can profit from it at this point?"

Discussion—Not Debate

Sooner or later you will find a person who argues (defends a predetermined position) rather than discusses (working with a group in order to develop more understanding than each possesses alone). Handling the person who grabs more than his share of the discussion can be ticklish. It is not wise, in the long run, to crack down on this person too early. If he continues to abuse his privilege, other members will probably soon become annoyed and make some remark. Then you have the "in" for speaking up in the interest of all participants in the discussion. You might say something like, "Perhaps, it would be best if we worked out a method for taking turns at speaking."

Unavailable Facts

It may also happen that certain facts not given by the case reports are asked for by group members. It's best not to make up facts. Reply to requests for other facts with statements such as: "How would it help you if you knew?" or "You have to work with the information given," or "Is that relevant to the question you are working on?" or "Even the experts are not in agreement on that."

Asking Questions

Much of the success of the course will depend upon your ability to ask questions. Your questions should be short and clearly phrased. Once the discussion has started, one of the best questions is, "Why?" Another good question is, "Mr. ————'s position seems to be that ————. Well, then, is not the problem we have to get into (insert here one of the discussion points)?"

New conference leaders often worry about how to include all the discussion points in the discussion. You may find yourself worrying about what question to ask next while another question is under discussion. The way to avoid this worry is to listen and think with the group. If you do this thinking and listening, natural openings will occur into which you can inject the right question. Careful listening and thought will tell you *when* to ask *what*.

The Silent Participant

The other extreme from the person who hogs the discussion is the member who never talks at all. Some effort should be made to encourage these people to participate in the discussion. However, if reasonable efforts are not successful, the matter should not be pushed. Some people may attend the sessions, participate in the huddles, think with the group, follow the arguments, and refuse to contribute anything at all. These people can benefit from the discussions even though they refuse to say anything.

On the other hand, some silent members will speak up if given assistance or encouragement. Occasionally, by watching the face of such a person, you will be able to know when he has something on the tip of his tongue. At this point, ask him whether he would like to add something.

It is sometimes a good idea to speak to the silent member privately. Try to discover what is holding him back. Ask him whether he wants to be called on next time. It may be that his sentiments are out of harmony with the group. Tell him that this is acceptable and that by not receiving his views all members are suffering. Tell him that if he wants to speak to give you a little signal and that he will get the floor. If he just does not want to speak, don't press him. Gently encourage him from time to time and when he is ready to speak he will join on his own accord.

Other techniques for drawing out the reluctant team member include appointing him as team leader for the huddle, asking him to prepare a method for evaluating the progress of the class, asking him to give a summary of the discussion, or asking him to prepare a constructive analysis of the procedures and suggestions for improvement.

The Explorer

An easier type of participant to manage is the explorer. He starts on one point, wanders to another, explores some unrelated information, goes up a side road and finally forgets the point he set out to make. This is more frequently found in early sessions and is found more often in persons who are unaccustomed to critical thinking. Often these people have many thoughts they wish to make at once and are unable to make a selection from them.

One technique for keeping the explorer on the track is to direct the question on the floor to a participant who you know gives short, direct replies. The contrast between the direct reply and the reply of the explorer may help the explorer to see how he might have answered in a more clear-cut manner. Another stronger method is to remark, "I seem to have lost you, Mr. ─────; I'm not able to see how your remarks relate to the question."

Patriotism

In police circles conformity to the group opinion is often considered to be the equivalent of national patriotism. Thus, if the group has leaned away from the human relations point of view, the minority may not speak up. The chairman may occasionally have to take up the minority point of view. Be sure that the human relations point of view is given serious consideration in every discussion. It's up to you to keep the course moving toward its objectives. You can always say, "Couldn't someone argue this way?" and then positively present one of the "Discussion Points" or "Lead Questions" related to the non-considered arguments. This may also encourage other group members, who hold minority points of view, to enter into the discussion. Once they enter the discussion, you can withdraw to your role of an impartial chairman.

Those Who Don't Seem to Get the Message

It is not to be expected that all members of every group will completely get the message. Certainly the type of material that you will be trying to put across is difficult to transfer at best. It may not be until the last two or three meetings that any progress whatsoever is noticed. However, with most group members some progress will be noted by the third to the fifth meetings. On the basis of your observations in class, you may decide that certain individuals are not making any progress at all. These persons should be scheduled for a separate meeting with the social science resource person and you. In this meeting, perhaps you can uncover the stumbling block and start this person down the road.

Role Playing in Meetings Four and Eight

Meetings four and eight are based on the role playing technique. You will find it necessary to introduce the role playing with a few introductory remarks. These remarks should be something like this: "Today we are going to vary the procedure slightly. Instead of giving you a scenario and following the usual plan, we are going to do some play acting. I'll read a description of an incident to you; then I'll assign roles for certain ones of you to play. There is no script. You just play the role the way that you think the character you are playing would act. Say and do exactly what you think the character would do and say.

"After each scene, we'll discuss the action. OK? Is there any incipient John Barrymore here? Who wants the woman's role?"

Further directions for carrying out the role playing are found with the materials for meetings four and eight. A discussion will be held of each role playing scene and the "Discussion Points" and "Lead Questions" are handled just as you would in any of the other discussions. Of course, in these role playing periods, there will be no huddle question assignments to subgroups.

Final Words

If you've read this far and have already completed the training for conference leaders (or are going to receive this training in the near future) you have little to worry about. However, no co-chairman, no matter how adequately he has prepared, will meet any group without some stage fright. If you are going to worry, be sure to worry about proper things. Things to worry about are:

    1. Including in the discussion as many as possible of the "discussion points."

2. Having your summaries properly reflect the course objectives.
3. Maintaining a democratic atmosphere in which everyone has the right to speak and to his own opinion.
4. Drawing out the shrinking violet and assuring that a verbal bully doesn't dominate any group.
5. Reaching the course objectives for the most people.
6. Failure if it's your fault.
7. Leading without lecturing.
8. Keeping your questions brief and to the point.
9. Allowing all group members to participate.
10. Interrupting a good, relevant discussion to introduce a new point.
11. Talking too much.

Things *not* to worry about are:

1. Whether group opinion at the outset is in harmony with human relations frame of reference of the course.
2. Whether your superiors are behind you—they are.
3. Disappointments.
4. What went wrong last time.
5. Failure if it's not your fault.
6. Listening too much and talking too little.

SECTION II
CASE AND ROLE PLAYING MATERIALS

CASE I—STREET LOUNGING
STAGE 1—INITIAL ENTRY

Group Material

On a hot, humid summer night, at 12:30 a.m., Officers Johnson and Romanowicz, while on squad car patrol, observed a crowd of seven to eight men on a corner across the street from the Silver Dollar Bar and Grill. The neighborhood in which the bar is located is composed of low income families who live in small, six-room row houses. Many are privately owned; others are rented at nominal rates. Since the congregants seemed to be loud and boisterous, the police officers stopped their car near the crowd of men. The men, in their late twenties to early thirties, seemed to be casually clothed; they wore light weight cotton trousers and tee shirts. One man stood out in the crowd. He seemed somewhat older than the others and was wearing a light tropical suit, a white shirt buttoned at the collar, a tie, and a panama hat.

Officer Romanowicz leaned out of the car window and asked the group not to congregate on the street. Although none of the residents in the neighborhood had complained to the police, Officer Romanowicz further stated that the police had received a complaint.

The men did not say anything to the officers. However, they displayed their annoyance and belligerence toward the officer's request in the manner in which they walked away and by the expressions on their faces.

HUDDLE QUESTIONS FOR "STREET LOUNGING"— "INITIAL ENTRY"

Group A: Some experts maintain that certain environmental factors lead to behavior such as street lounging. What might these be and what other reasons can you offer explaining why people may congregate on streets?

DISCUSSION POINTS FOR "STREET LOUNGING"—"INITIAL ENTRY"

Attitudes	Knowledges	Skills
How a person's "present mood" determines how he will react to other people	Why street corner loungers may be reluctant to disperse	Asking a group of street corner loungers to disperse
	Why some people feel abused or "picked on" by the police	Dispersing a group of street corner loungers
	Why some people possess an arrogant attitude toward the police	Explaining the law to people
	The ways in which certain people think	Making quick decisions on a course of action to follow
	The sense of values that people possess	Taking action that you think your supervisors would want you to take
	Ethics and professionalism in police work	
	The civil rights laws	

Given the same environmental factors, would all people act the same? Is it within the rights of citizens to congregate on street corners? Why are street loungers often reluctant to disperse?

Group B: Were Officers Johnson and Romanowicz within their rights when they asked the group to disperse? Justify your answer. Would you, in a similar situation, explain the reason for your request to the street loungers? Was it proper for Officer Romanowicz to tell the street loungers that one of the nearby residents had complained? What are the possible consequences of such a lie?

LEAD QUESTIONS FOR "STREET LOUNGING"— "INITIAL ENTRY"

1. How could popular magazines and newspapers have contributed to the attitude shown toward the police by the loungers?
2. Do you think that street loungers view themselves as violators of the law?
3. Could personality mechanisms such as repressed tensions and frustrations be expressing themselves in the behaviors of the loungers?
4. How does frustration manifest itself in such behaviors as: (a) crime and radicalism, (b) aggression against authority, (c) self punishment, (d) group identification?
5. Could the dress of the loungers be interpreted as a prestige symbol similar to the yacht of the businessman or the political leanings of some college students? How so?
6. Should police officers explain to street loungers why they are asking them to disperse? Why?

CASE I—STREET LOUNGING
STAGE 2—FACT FINDING

Group Material

Officers Johnson and Romanowicz continued on their patrol. About half an hour later, while driving along the same street, they noticed the same group of men congregated in exactly the same place.

The officers approached the group. This second time the officers were less courteous and, on the hunch that the men were congregating for other than social reasons, ordered the men to line up against the wall so that a search could be performed. The older, very nattily dressed man, who appeared to be the leader of the group, objected to this treatment. He claimed that no one had done any wrong and that the police had no right to treat the group "like common criminals." The officers just ignored his comments, shoved him toward the wall, and said, "Come on, just get your hands up on the wall."

As the men lined up against the wall, one of them put a brown bag on the ground between his feet. Officer Johnson opened the bag and found a half empty bottle of bourbon. The bottle did not have a state tax seal on it. He took the bottle and exclaimed, "Just as I thought, they've been drinking." Turning to the owner of the liquor, Officer Johnson said, "What's the matter, bud, you bringing in the holiday a little early?"

Officer Romanowicz frisked the apparent leader and found a knife in his pants pocket. The man tried to offer an explanation, but Romanowicz told him to "save it until you get down to the station house." The men were also asked for their draft cards. A review of the cards showed that the men were all over twenty-one years of age.

While the street loungers were standing with their hands against the wall, one of them became very belligerent. In a very hostile tone he said, "You God damn cops are all alike. Put a uniform on you and you think you're a king."

HUDDLE QUESTIONS FOR "STREET LOUNGING"— "FACT FINDING"

Group A: Do you think that the officers should have employed the same politeness the second time as they did when they first encountered the loungers? Why? When is a street search proper? Justify your answer. Was it proper in this case? On the basis of the facts given, what course of action do you think the officers should now take?

DISCUSSION POINTS FOR "STREET LOUNGING"—"FACT FINDING"

Attitudes	Knowledges	Skills
How a person's "present mood" will determine how he will react to other people	Why some people feel abused or "picked on" by the police	Being polite to people when interrogating them
	The sense of values that people possess	Explaining the law to people
	The dynamics of human personality	Trying to pacify a person
	The civil rights laws	Explaining to a person the reasons for frisking or searching him
	Ethics and professionalism in police work	Explaining the constitutional rights to a citizen
		Taking into consideration the fact that people are not aware that they violated the law before deciding upon what action to take toward them
		Searching a person
		Taking action you think your supervisors would want you to take
		Tolerating verbal abuse

Group B: Why might people such as the loungers gravitate toward each other in small groups? Consider and report on your impressions of the effects of: (1) the tendency of others to "put minorities in their place," (2) lack of steady jobs, (3) lack of social belongingness to society in general, (4) individual prestige.

LEAD QUESTIONS FOR "STREET LOUNGING"— "FACT FINDING"

1. Certain ladies try to keep up with the latest book recommended by the book club; others feel they will be left out if they are not up-to-date in the latest fashions. What similarities exist between the causes of these behaviors and that of the street loungers?
2. Why do you think the street lounger who said, "Put a uniform on and you think you're a king," denounced the police? How should an officer react to such a comment? How would your superior officers want you to react?
3. How do you think most people feel about bringing out-of-state liquor into a state? Do you think they regard themselves as criminals? Why?
4. Do you think that the older street lounger's comment that the group shouldn't be treated "like common criminals" was justifiable? Should this remark have been answered by the police? If so, how might it have been answered?

CASE I—STREET LOUNGING
STAGE 3—CONSUMMATING THE PLAN

Group Material

As Officer Johnson returned to the patrol car to call for a wagon, the older man called out to him, "Officer, can't you forget this matter? We really weren't doing anything illegal. We were just standing here and talking." Officer Johnson replied, "Look, we gave you your chance; now you're going to have to explain it to the lieutenant."

The belligerent street lounger then yelled out, "What the hell are you trying to explain to them for? They don't care if we're guilty of anything as long as they can impress their boss."

Officer Romanowicz pointed his finger at the man and said, "We've taken enough crap from you. Now just stand there and relax. Save your energy. You're going to have a lot of explaining to do."

Several minutes later the wagon arrived. The street loungers were ushered into the wagon and taken to district headquarters.

When they arrived at the station house, the street loungers were lined up in front of the desk. The lieutenant asked the first man for his name. This was the same hostile, belligerent man who had been abusive to the officers earlier. The man gave his name. When asked if he had ever been brought in before, he replied, "I'm not telling you a thing more."

Officer Romanowicz walked up to him, pushed him in the back and ordered, "Don't you try to be wise. Just answer his questions." With this, the street lounger turned around and yelled, "Keep your filthy hands off me!" As he spoke these words, he stepped back and kicked Officer Romanowicz in the groin. Officer Romanowicz doubled over in severe pain. Officer Johnson, who was standing nearby, then struck the lounger several times. As soon as he could, the lieutenant ordered Officer Johnson to stop.

Subsequently, the total group, with the exception of the man who was offensive, was released. The offensive lounger was held for court.

HUDDLE QUESTIONS FOR "STREET LOUNGING"— "CONSUMMATING THE PLAN"

Group A: Should the police officers have taken the group to the station house? How do you think other citizens would react to this incident if they heard about it? How important is it for an officer to be concerned with the general reactions of other citizens?

Group B: How might the offensive street lounger have been better handled? Do you think that Officer Romanowicz's behavior was wise? Is it a good idea to show authority in order to impress or frighten?

Discussion Points for "Street Lounging" — "Consummating the Plan"

Attitudes	Knowledges	Skills	Decisions
Why people may verbally abuse an officer	Why some people feel abused or "picked on" by the police	Determining whether or not a person is telling the truth	To book or not to book someone
Why some people are not aware that they violated the law	Why some people possess an arrogant attitude toward the police	Deciding why a person may be lying	That sufficient and legitimate cause for police action does or does not exist
How a person's "present mood" determines how he will react to other people	The ways in which certain people think	Deciding if a crime has been committed	To caution someone about his actions
Why officers may take out their gripes on the public	The sense of values that people possess	Considering all possible complications if an arrest is made	To offer advice
	The points of view that different people have on a given issue	Making quick decisions on a course of action to follow	To ignore or not to ignore verbal abuse
	The dynamics of human personality	Cautioning a person against the use of obscene language	That whether a person was or was not telling the truth
	The civil rights laws	Tolerating verbal abuse	To show authority or to threaten with intent to impress or frighten
	Ethics and professionalism in police work	Trying to pacify a person	To ignore an offender's excuse for a misdemeanor
	Why street corner loungers may be reluctant to disperse	Answering coherent questions politely	To refuse a person's request

LEAD QUESTIONS FOR "STREET LOUNGING"— "CONSUMMATING THE PLAN"

1. How did the police officers show a lack of professionalism in this incident? How would you have handled it and why?
2. Why is it important for officers to control their behavior and not become hostile or belligerent toward citizens? How do you think your supervisors would answer this question?
3. If released, do you think the loungers would repeat this type of behavior or do you think that the individuals will be less apt to lounge on the street corners in the future? Why?
4. Discuss the relationship between "educational failure" and the behavior of the loungers.
5. What will the loungers likely be thinking after they leave the station house?
6. Should an arrest have been made in this situation? If yes, on what grounds? If no, why? How do you think the public or the press might react if the arrested man is found innocent and released?

CASE II—HOUSE SEARCH
STAGE 1—INITIAL ENTRY

Group Material

On April 16, plain-clothes Detectives Adams (Negro) and Harris (white) entered the home of Mr. and Mrs. Frank Gagliardi in order to search the Gagliardi residence. The neighborhood had recently become integrated and some hostility toward their Negro neighbors existed in certain of the white residents. The police had received a "tip" from an informant that the Gagliardis were operating a gambling house.

Mr. and Mrs. Gagliardi, who were eating lunch, heard their door bell and the stimultaneous opening of their front door. Both saw Detective Adams walking through the house. Adams was approached in the dining room by Mrs. Gagliardi, who belligerently asked, "What are you doing in my house?" Since the detective, dressed in plain clothes, had admitted himself, Mrs. Gagliardi assumed that he was a burglar. Mrs. Gagliardi was aware of several recent crimes in the neighborhood that were reported as committed by Negroes.

Detective Adams said, "We are police officers. We got a tip that this is a gambling house." At this point, Mr. Gagliardi came in and yelled, "What's going on here? What right do you have breaking into our home and accusing us of operating a gambling house?"

Harris, who had now entered the room, said, "Come clean. We know you write numbers. We're going to search this house." He reached into his pocket, pulled out some folded papers, and said, "We have a warrant to search the house right here." He motioned to the papers and replaced them in his pocket.

Mrs. Gagliardi, raising her voice excitedly, said, "What kind of tip could you have? Do you think my door would be left open if this was a gambling house? I don't want you fellows in my house—you're invading my privacy—*I won't let you* search the house!" Detective Adams said, "Look, lady, what are you getting so excited about if you're not guilty?" She replied, "What am I getting so excited about? This is my house! I'm not accustomed to colored men opening my door and entering my house! How do I know who you are? Maybe you came here to attack me. There's a lot of Negroes committing crimes around this city, isn't there?" Detective Adams replied, "Yes, there is a lot of crime in this city—it's being committed by Negroes and whites—and Italians." To this, Mrs. Gagliardi replied, "You colored people commit crimes and then accuse the white people of doing the same thing and that makes you innocent."

HUDDLE QUESTIONS FOR "HOUSE SEARCH"— "INITIAL ENTRY"

Group A: If environment and education were equated, would the crime rate be the same for all racial and national groups? Is it expecting too much when we expect mixed races to live together peaceably?

Group B: How might Detective Adams have avoided arousing the anger of the Gagliardis? How could Detective Harris have avoided antagonizing the Gagliardis? Should police officers in such situations be concerned

DISCUSSION POINTS FOR "HOUSE SEARCH" — "INITIAL ENTRY"

Attitudes	Knowledges	Skills
How a person's "present mood" determines how he will react to other people	Why people object to having their homes searched	Entering a house harmoniously with a warrant
Why officers take out personal gripes on the public	Why some people possess arrogant attitudes toward the police	Explaining the purpose of your presence before taking action
	The sense of values that people possess	Tolerating verbal abuse
	The civil rights involved	Pacifying a person
		Answering coherent questions politely
		Explaining the law to a citizen
		Making quick decisions on a course of action
		Taking action your supervisors would want you to take
		Combatting false rumors

with the feelings and attitudes of the citizens involved or should they be primarily concerned with getting their job done (i.e., searching the house)? Why?

LEAD QUESTIONS FOR "HOUSE SEARCH"— "INITIAL ENTRY"

1. Why might Mr. and Mrs. Gagliardi have been belligerent to the police officers? Were the Gagliardis justified or unjustified in acting toward the police in this manner?
2. Why might members of minority groups develop feelings of persecution?
3. What, if anything, should Detective Adams have done before entering the house? Criticize his initial entry.
4. How might you have tried to pacify the Gagliardis when they were obviously hostile and uncooperative?
5. What should you do or say if you were Detective Adams and Mrs. Gagliardi told you that ". . . colored people commit crimes and then accuse the white people of doing the same thing and that makes you innocent?"
6. Does the fact that Mrs. Gagliardi mentioned that she was not accustomed to colored men entering her home unannounced indicate a prejudice against Negroes? How might such a feeling arise? Is it justified?
7. Did Detective Adams act wisely when he told Mrs. Gagliardi that crimes were being committed by Negroes, whites, and Italians? What should you do in this situation?

CASE II—HOUSE SEARCH
STAGE 2—FACT FINDING

Group Material

Adams explained, "We have to get on with the job and search the place." Mrs. Gagliardi showed him her pay check and explained, "With a pay check of $122.70 for the week, there is no reason why I would have to write numbers." She also told the detectives that her husband earned $80 to $90 per week.

Adams then proceeded upstairs, where he made a thorough search of the bedrooms. He went through every drawer and closet. In the process, he disarranged the contents. Detective Harris took Mr. Gagliardi (who had lost a leg in an automobile accident) upstairs into one of the bedrooms, where he made Mr. Gagliardi undress in order to search him thoroughly.

After the detectives completed a search which revealed no evidence of numbers writing, Harris questioned Mr. Gagliardi about the number of telephones in the house. The house, of the small row variety, had a telephone in the dining room, kitchen, and in one of the bedrooms. Mr. Gagliardi, who worked at home, explained that with only one leg he had difficulty getting around and he needed a telephone "nearby at all times."

At about this time, the telephone rang. Adams said, "There it is", and reached for the telephone. Mrs. Gagliardi dodged in front of the officer exclaiming, "You have no right to answer my telephone!" The officer shoved her aside and answered the phone. It was the Gagliardi's married daughter.

HUDDLE QUESTIONS FOR "HOUSE SEARCH"— "FACT FINDING"

Group A: Why might people resent a search? Consider negativism in general, loss of prestige in the community, social self-respect, and pride in one's home "as his castle."

Group B: "Fixation" is a term applied to persisting in a form of behavior even after it has ceased to serve any purpose. Did the detectives demonstrate this type of behavior? Where else might it occur in police work?

LEAD QUESTIONS FOR "HOUSE SEARCH"— "FACT FINDING"

1. Was Detective Adams justified in answering the telephone? How would most citizens have interpreted this act?
2. What would you have done when the phone rang? Why?
3. Do you think the Gagliardis showed arrogance toward the police? Why might some people possess arrogant attitudes toward the police?
4. In what ways did Detectives Adams and Harris show a lack

DISCUSSION POINTS FOR "HOUSE SEARCH"—"FACT FINDING"

Attitudes	Knowledges	Skills
How a person's "present mood" determines how he will react to other people	Why people may feel they are being "picked on" by the police	Respecting the property of others when searching a house
Why officers take out their personal gripes on the public	The ways in which people think	Tolerating verbal abuse
	The sense of values that people possess	Refraining from verbally abusing a person
	Why people have different points of view on given issues	Being polite and courteous to people when interrogating them
	The dynamics of personality	Being patient with people when interrogating them
	Professionalism and ethics in police work	Explaining the law to people
		Pacifying a person
		Explaining the reasons for searching and frisking a person
		Answering coherent questions politely
		Taking actions your supervisors would want you to take
		Being firm with people and not granting them any special favors despite their background hardships

of respect for the personal property of the Gagliardis? How
should they have conducted the search?

5. How would you have felt if you were Mrs. Gagliardi? Mr.
Gagliardi? In view of Mr. Gagliardi's physical condition,
should the officers have offered him any special consideration?

CASE II—HOUSE SEARCH
STAGE 3—DECISION MAKING

Group Material

Adams and Harris found no evidence which indicated that any
gambling was being carried out in the home. Harris apologized
and explained that he understood the embarrassment and humili-
ation the Gagliardis had suffered as a result of being falsely
accused. They further explained that the police have a job to do
and that they are "trying to clean the city of the numbers racket
for the good of everyone." Consequently, when they were informed that the Gagliardis were operating a gambling house,
they "came over to collect any information we could to make an
arrest."

The detectives excused themselves and left.

HUDDLE QUESTIONS FOR "HOUSE SEARCH"—
"DECISION MAKING"

Group A: Do you think the Gagliardis objected specifically to
the treatment received from Detectives Adams and
Harris or do you think they were displaying a general,
free floating objection to authority?

Group B: How do you think the Gagliardis felt after this incident? What do you suppose their reactions toward
the police department might be? Do you think they
might feel that they were abused by the police department? Why? Are they justified in their feelings?

LEAD QUESTIONS FOR "HOUSE SEARCH"—
"DECISION MAKING"

1. What should the detectives have done or said after they

DISCUSSION POINTS FOR "HOUSE SEARCH" — "DECISION MAKING"

Attitudes	Knowledges	Skills	Decisions
How a person's "present mood" determines how he will react to other people	Why people object to having their homes searched	Determining if a person is telling the truth	Determining if a person is telling the truth
Why officers take out their personal gripes on the public	Why people feel they are being abused by the police	Deciding why a person may be lying	Deciding why a person may be lying
	Why people possess arrogant attitudes toward police	Deciding upon a course of action to follow	Deciding upon a course of action to follow
	Why people have different points of view on a given issue	Deciding if a crime has been committed	Deciding if a crime has been committed
	The dynamics of personality	Considering the complications that might arise if an arrest is made	Considering the complications that might arise if an arrest is made
	Professionalism and ethics in police work	Being firm with people and not granting them any special favors despite their background hardships	Being firm with people and not granting them any special favors despite their background hardships
		Confiscating personal property	Confiscating personal property
		Trying to reduce racial tension	Trying to reduce racial tension
		Combatting false rumors	Combatting false rumors

searched the house and found no evidence that the Gagliardis were operating a gambling house?

2. Would the Gagliardis have been more cooperative if other approaches and tactics had been used by the officers? What approach and tactics might have been used?

3. Could the police officers have offered the Gagliardis any advice so as to prevent the recurrence of such an incident? Should they offer this advice without being asked for it by the Gagliardis? What might this advice be?

CASE III—MOLESTING A FEMALE
STAGE 1—INITIAL ENTRY

Group Material

Officers Turman (Negro) and Christensen (white) were slowly cruising in a squad car at 1:30 a.m., on December 17. They noticed a squabble on the next corner.

On approaching the scene, the officers saw a white man, in his early to middle thirties, dragging a young Negro woman by the arm. The woman was struggling and kept slipping. A car, with an open door, was parked at the curb.

The police officers drove to the corner, stopped their squad car, and ran towards the couple. Officer Turman separated the couple. The officer grasped the man who offered no resistance to the police officers. It was obvious that the Negro woman was drunk—she was having difficulty standing without support and was mumbling incoherently.

HUDDLE QUESTIONS FOR "MOLESTING A FEMALE"— "INITIAL ENTRY"

Group A: Just as white men have the right to prefer plump women to lean women, they also have the right to prefer Negro women to white women. True or false. Why?

Group B: What cultural factors play a significant role in the development of how we interpret what we see? How might the background of Turman and Christensen

DISCUSSION POINTS FOR "MOLESTING A FEMALE"—"INITIAL ENTRY"

Attitudes	Knowledges	Skills
How a person's "present mood" determines how he will react to other people	Why some people possess an arrogant attitude toward the police	Preventing a woman from being molested
Why officers take their personal gripes out on the public	The way people think	Not assuming that a woman is being molested even though she may be struggling with a man
	The sense of values that certain people possess	Explaining the law to people
	The civil rights laws	Trying to pacify a person
	Prejudice, its nature and derivation	Making quick decisions on a course of action to follow
	Ethics and professionalism in police work	Taking actions that you think your supervisors would want you to take

have caused each of them to interpret this incident differently?

LEAD QUESTIONS FOR "MOLESTING A FEMALE"— "INITIAL ENTRY"

1. Do you think that members of minority groups discriminate against non-members? If yes, how do you think this type of prejudice develops?
2. How is sexual behavior influenced by culture as embodied in the social structure?
3. How does the church feel about intergroup marriages?

CASE III—MOLESTING A FEMALE
STAGE 2—FACT FINDING

Group Material

Officer Turman helped the Negro woman into the back of the squad car. He returned to Officer Christensen, who was interrogating the man. The interrogation revealed that the man was not trying to molest the woman. Rather, he was attempting to get her into his car so that he could take her home. Furthermore, the couple had been living together as common-law husband and wife for the past three years. The man, Carter Lamont, was an artist who worked independently. The couple lived in his apartment which was located seven blocks from the place of the incident. Lamont also had his studio in the apartment.

That evening, Lamont had gone out on a business call. He had returned at about 10:30 and did not find his "wife" at home. He waited until midnight, and when the woman did not return, Lamont decided to go out to look for her. He thought that she might have gone to one of the several tap rooms which they often frequented. He found her in a bar which was close to the current scene.

On finding his "wife," Lamont had picked up her coat, grabbed her by the arm, and attempted to lead her out of the bar and into the car. She put up a feeble struggle, and when the police arrived on the scene, was objecting to entering the car.

Discussion Points for "Molesting a Female"—"Fact Finding"

Attitudes	Knowledges	Skills
How a person's "present mood" will determine how he will react to others	The way people think	Determining whether a woman is being molested before taking any action against the man
Why some officers take out their personal gripes on the public	The sense of values that people possess	Interrogating a man for his side of the story
	The dynamics of personality	Being polite to people when interrogating them
	The civil rights laws	Being patient when interrogating people
	Ethics and professionalism in police work	Determining whether an incident between whites and non-whites was caused by racial differences
	The living conditions of various ethnic groups	Taking actions that you think your supervisors would want you to take
	All members of minority groups are neither good nor bad	Determining the severity of a person's injury
	What a person's point of view is on a given issue	

HUDDLE QUESTIONS FOR "MOLESTING A FEMALE"— "FACT FINDING"

Group A: Do you think that this case, because it involves an interracial situation, involves considerations which would not be involved if the couple were members of the same race? If yes, how so?

Group B: Should an incident involving a common-law husband and wife relationship receive different treatment from one involving a legally married couple? If so, how?

LEAD QUESTIONS FOR "MOLESTING A FEMALE"— "FACT FINDING"

1. How do you react to Carter Lamont? Is he a socially acceptable or socially unacceptable person? Why?
2. Do you think the police officers should have investigated the female involved in this incident? What should they be concerned with as far as she is concerned?
3. Why are common-law marriages frowned upon?
4. What would you do now if you were one of the officers involved?

CASE III—MOLESTING A FEMALE
STAGE 3—DECISION MAKING

Group Material

When Carter Lamont finished telling Officers Turman and Christensen his story, Officer Christensen said, "Let's get her story." On returning to the squad car, the officers found the woman fast asleep. They tried to awaken her but could not; she was too drunk.

Officer Turman then turned to the man and said, "Well, we're going to have to lock you up tonight. There's no way we can tell if your story is true." The officers put Carter Lamont in the squad car and drove to the station house.

HUDDLE QUESTIONS FOR "MOLESTING A FEMALE"— "DECISION MAKING"

Group A: What other avenues might have been pursued in

DISCUSSION POINTS FOR "MOLESTING A FEMALE" — "DECISION MAKING"

Attitudes	Knowledges	Skills	Decisions
How a person's "present mood" determines how he will react to others	Why some people may feel "picked on" by the police	Making quick decisions on a course of action to follow	To book or not book someone
Why police officers take out personal gripes on the public	The way people think	Treating more educated people differently than less educated people	That sufficient and legitimate cause for police action does or does not exist
	The sense of values that people possess	Preventing a woman from being molested	To caution someone about his actions
	A person's point of view on a given issue	Cautioning a man that his actions toward a woman could be interpreted to mean that he was molesting her	To offer advice
	The cultures of minority groups	Arresting a man for molesting a woman	To obtain information of a non routine nature
	What type of action would your supervisors want you to take		That medical attention was or was not needed
	The civil rights laws		That a person was or was not telling the truth
	Ethics and professionalism in police work		To ignore the offender's excuse for a misdemeanor

trying to determine the truthfulness of the Lamont story?

Group B: Do you think that the fact that a white man was living with a Negro woman negatively disposed the police officers toward the man? Should police officers try to avoid letting such feelings influence their actions?

LEAD QUESTIONS FOR "MOLESTING A FEMALE"— "DECISION MAKING"

1. Do you think the police officers were justified or unjustified in booking Lamont? Why?
2. If you were offering Lamont any advice as a result of this incident, what might you tell him?

CASE IV—CAR STOP
ROLE PLAY INSTRUCTIONS
Conference Leader Instructions

Procedure

1. Read the *Introduction and Background* to the case to the group.

2. Ask for volunteers for the roles of
   a. Police Officer Rossi
   b. Police Officer Gardner
   c. The Negro man
   d. The woman

The role players need not be members of the same race or sex as called for in the case material. If no one volunteers for the roles, select four people.

3. Allow each player to read only the instructions for his own role. Do not pass the role material to the rest of the group. Allow the players enough time to read and understand their roles.

4. Provide the props for the players. Only two chairs, two pads, and two pencils are necessary. Place the chairs side by side. They represent the front seat of the automobile in which the man and woman are seated. The pads and pencils are for Officers Rossi and Gardner.

5. When the players are ready, ask them to take their places. The man and woman are to be seated. The woman is seated to the right of the man as she would be in an automobile which the man is driving. Officer Rossi is standing alongside the man and Officer Gardner is off to the side.

6. There is no specified time limit, but stop each stage after 15 minutes if the role playing extends that long.

7. After the role playing for this stage has terminated, give the players their role material for the second stage and read the *Introduction* to that stage to the group. After the second stage has terminated, give the players their role material for the last stage.

8. When the last stage is finished, conduct the discussion with the entire group. There will be no "huddles." During the discussion be sure to allow the actors to save face by stating their reactions and why they responded as they did.

CASE IV—CAR STOP
STAGE 1—INITIAL ENTRY

Introduction and Background

On July 10, at 10:00 p.m., Officers Rossi and Gardner, both white, are on a routine patrol in their squad car in a district which is almost exclusively Negro. The district is characterized by a high crime rate and general unrest. Solid police work is continually required to keep this district orderly. The district is particularly difficult on hot summer nights when the residents leave their apartments and congregate on the steps, in the streets, and in bars where they often becom boistrous and unruly.

The evening is hot and a general alert is out for a Negro prowler who had molested several women and children in the neighborhood. It is known that the prowler drives a blue 1959 Chevrolet sedan. The license number of the car is not known. In spite of the best efforts of the police, no success has been achieved in apprehending the prowler. Considerable top-side pressure has been brought to bear in solving this case. The officers on their tour have made several routine car searches and accosted one traffic violator. Otherwise, the tour has been without incident.

Discussion Points for "Car Stop"—"Initial Entry"

Attitudes	Knowledges	Skills
Why a motorist may be angry when his car is stopped	The civil rights involved	Employing the unique slang used by people when talking with them
How a person's "present mood" determines how he will react to others	What causes racial tension	Explaining to a motorist that he is not being "picked on" because of his skin color or for other reasons
Why an officer may take out his personal gripes on the public	An understanding of the cultures of minority groups	Explaining to a motorist the reasons for making a "routine car stop"
Why some people may feel abused or "picked on" by the police	The sense of values that people possess	Approaching and talking to motorists in a polite manner
	How people think	Determining whether or not a motorist has committed a violation of the motor vehicle code
	Why some people possess an arrogant attitude toward the police	Tolerating verbal abuse
		Explaining the law to people
		Trying to pacify a person
		Answering coherent questions
		Explaining the constitutional rights to a citizen
		Taking into consideration the fact that some people are not aware that they violated the law before deciding upon what action to take towards them
		Taking action that you think your supervisors would want you to take

　　The officers decide to stop and search a Ford sedan in which
· a well-dressed Negro man and woman are riding. They flag the
car to the curb and Rossi approaches the car to interrogate the
couple while Gardner remains in the squad car.

Role of Officer Rossi

　　You have flagged the car to a stop. Approach the driver and
politely state that you are performing a routine check. Remain
polite but insist upon checking the driver's license and registration. The female passenger, who is obviously high, but not
drunk, may be hard to handle. But you have your duty to
perform.

Role of Officer Gardner

　　Remain off to the side. If Officer Rossi seems to be having
difficulty, enter the case and see what you can do. If you enter
the case, be short and abusive to the couple. Use terms and
phrases such as "Knock off that shit," "Don't give us any lip," and
"We've got good ways to take care of wise guys." Refer to the
driver as "boy" when you tell him not to give you any trouble.

Role of Negro Man

　　You are stopped by police officers who want to make a
routine check. You are sitting behind the wheel of your car.
You are polite and accommodating but anxious to know why the
police are investigating your car. You are concerned about this
police check and you keep stressing that you haven't done anything wrong. Don't show the officers your cards. Remain polite
but refuse to show your cards.

　　Officer Gardner, who may be abusive toward you, may call
you "boy." If he does, object to this; tell him that your name
isn't "boy" and tell him that you are not trying to cause any
trouble—you just want to know what you've done. Be sure to
remember to try to be polite at all times.

Role of Female Passenger

　　You are high from drinking. Be very abusive toward the
police officers. You don't like the police. You think car searches
are unconstitutional and that the police pick on people. Let

the police know this and let them know that you think that they have no right to interrogate you. This is the opportunity you have been waiting for. Don't let your companion show the police a thing and try not to let him answer their questions. Remember to defend your rights at all times.

Keep interrupting the officers and your companion to get your points across. If the officers don't listen to you or ignore you, gain their attention by telling them to "go to hell," "kiss my ass," etc.

CASE IV—CAR STOP
STAGE 2—FACT FINDING

Introduction

Officer Gardner insists that the couple get out of their car. They oblige. The police officers continue their investigation.

Role of Officer Rossi

Remain polite but stern throughout the investigation despite the opposition of the woman. Your investigation primarily pertains to establishing the identity and integrity of the occupants of the car. You will do most of the questioning. Ask: Are you married? Where do you live? Where have you been? Where are you going? What do you do for a living? How long have you lived in this city? Ask any other related questions you think important.

Insist on seeing the man's license and registration.

Role of Officer Gardner

Allow Officer Rossi to do most of the questioning. Remain very hostile toward the couple and especially to the woman. Tell the couple to get out of the car. At one point, after she has made a comment which arouses your hostility, blurt out, "You damn people are all the same."

Role of Negro Man

You are still polite and cooperative. Answer all questions but one. The one question you refuse to answer pertains to your

Discussion Points for "Car Stop"—"Fact Finding"

Attitudes	Knowledges	Skills
Why a motorist may become hostile when interrogated	Why a motorist may be reluctant to produce his driver's license and car registration	Asking for a driver's license, car registration, and any other identification information
How a person's "present mood" determines how he will react to others	Why a motorist may refuse to answer some questions	Interrogating a suspicious motorist
Why an officer may take out his personal gripes on the public	The dynamics of human personality	Explaining to a motorist that he is not being "picked on" because of the color of his skin or for other reasons
	The civil rights laws	Tolerating verbal abuse
	Ethics and professionalism in police work	Being polite to people when interrogating them
	Why some people feel abused or "picked on"	Being patient when interrogating people
		Explaining the law to people
		Trying to pacify a person

relationship to the woman. When the officers ask you about this relationship, refuse to answer by stating that it's personal business and that you are within your rights not to answer.

Allow the officers to uncover the facts that you moved to this city several months ago and that you are a construction worker. In this stage, allow the officers to see your out-of-state operator's license. Provide the following information to the officers. You have no registration card for the car. As far as you know, the car belongs to the woman. You had arrangements to meet her after work in a bar near your job. When you got there she was a little tipsy so you decided to drive her home. That is where you were going when the police stopped you. After you got her to her home, you were going to take a taxi back to your apartment.

At one point during the investigation make an offer of money to the officers, provided they forget the incident.

Role of Female Passenger

Remain extremely belligerent towards the officers. Tell them that they have no right to keep picking on you. Although the investigation is primarily concerned with your male companion, keep interrupting with hostile remarks. After your male companion has answered the officer's questions as to who he is and where he lives, interject a statement such as, "We told you who we are and where we live and that's all we're going to tell you. If that isn't enough for you, take us down to the station house." If your companion wants to, let him show his operator's license during this stage.

CASE IV—CAR STOP
STAGE 3—DECISION MAKING

Role of Officer Rossi

Make an appropriate decision and close out the case. Confer with Officer Gardner if you wish.

Role of Officer Gardner

Officer Rossi will make the decision on how to dispose of the

DISCUSSION POINTS FOR "CAR STOP"—"DECISION MAKING"

Attitudes	Knowledges	Skills	Decisions
Why people verbally abuse police officers	Why some people are not aware that they violated the law	Explaining to a motorist that he is not being "picked on" because of the color of his skin or for other reasons	To book or not to book someone
How a person's "present mood" determines how he will react to others	Why motorists refuse to answer an officer's questions	Determining if a motorist has committed a violation of the motor vehicle code	To ticket or not to ticket a motorist
	The dynamics of personality	Determining whether or not a person is telling the truth	That sufficient and legitimate cause for police action does or does not exist
	The civil rights laws	Deciding why a person may be lying	To caution someone about his actions
	Prejudice, its nature and derivation	Taking into consideration the fact that some people are not aware that they violated the law before deciding upon what action to take towards them	To offer advice
	Ethics and professionalism in police work	Deciding whether or not a crime has been committed	To ignore or not ignore verbal abuse
	All members of minority groups are neither good nor bad	Making quick decisions on a course of action to follow	To obtain information of a non routine nature
		Explaining to a motorist why he is being given a ticket	That the person was or was not telling the truth
		Trying to pacify a person	To ignore an offender's excuse for a misdemeanor
		Arresting people for disorderly conduct (loud and/or obscene language)	To refuse a person's request

case. Agree with his decision. Say whatever you feel is appropriate.

Role of Negro Man

You are cooperative and polite throughout this stage. After the officers come to their decision, make no comment and cooperate.

Role of Female Passenger

Remain hostile towards the police officers. After the officers come to their decision, continue with your sarcastic remarks.

LEAD QUESTIONS FOR "CAR STOP"—"INITIAL ENTRY"

1. Criticize the initial entry of the officers.
2. How do you think you would feel in this situation if you were the Negro man? Why do you think you would feel this way?
3. If you were Officer Rossi, what would you do if such language were directed at you? Do you think your actions would be justified? Why might they be wrong?
4. How do you think Officer Gardner's behavior affected the situation?
5. Why might the woman have felt picked on? Why might she have been justified? Unjustified?
6. What could the officers have done or said to make the search proceed more smoothly?
7. Why do you think Officer Gardner was as abrupt as he was? Is it possible that something in his personal life might have caused this behavior?

LEAD QUESTIONS FOR "CAR STOP"—"FACT FINDING"

1. Why do you think the motorist was reluctant to reveal any information pertaining to his relationship to the woman? Was he within his rights?
2. Why do some people become hostile when they are interrogated by the police? How might this hostility be handled?
3. Do you think the woman would have been less offensive if she had not been under the influence of alcohol? How do you think her personality was affected by the liquor?

4. Did the officers display proper ethics and professionalism? Discuss their actions from this point of view.
5. Criticize Officer Gardner's approach and attitude in this stage.
6. How do you think prejudice affects the personality of the prejudiced person?
7. What role do you think parents play in transmitting prejudicial attitudes? Do you think there is a difference in the amount of prejudice found in different economic groups? How would this operate?
8. Do you think there is a relationship between prejudice and lack of education? Why? How might such a relationship come about?
9. It has been said by some people that the crime rate among Negro migrants is higher than it is for nonmigrants. Do you agree or disagree with this hypothesis? Support your conclusions.

LEAD QUESTIONS FOR "CAR STOP"—"DECISION MAKING"

1. How would you have handled the abusive woman in this incident? Why?
2. Was there legitimate and sufficient cause for police action? What do you think the officers should have done in this incident?
3. Do you think the officers should have considered the fact that the man was not aware that he was violating the law by driving without the registration? Why?
4. What advice would you have offered the couple, if any?

CASE V—CROWD
STAGE 1—INITIAL ENTRY

Group Material

Officers Llewelin and Morgan were riding in a squad car on September 8. At approximately 7:00 p.m., they noticed five Negro men standing in front of an apartment house. The Negro men looked suspicious—they were garbed in what may be described as self-styled religious robes. Although the men were only standing on the street, the police officers decided to ask the men to account for their presence. A spokesman for the five men explained to the officers that they were ———s (a small religious sect), and were waiting for two "sisters" who had gone into the apartment house "to make a religious solicitation." The officers decided to wait for the "sisters" to come out.

At this time, a third officer approached and asked what was going on. While producing the "credentials" of his sect, the leader became noticeably nervous. He explained that residents were only met with by appointment and that no door-to-door canvassing or solicitation was taking place.

The police officers doubted that these men were solely involved in religious solicitation. About fifteen minutes passed and the two "sisters" did not come out of the house. Officer Morgan became impatient and told the leader of the group, "I don't give a God damn what your purpose is. You're not supposed to solicit. If you were legitimate religious solicitors, you would know that you have to get an okay before you solicit. I think we'll take all of you in."

By this time, a sizable crowd (comprised primarily of Negroes from the neighborhood) had gathered. Two of the officers tried to break up the crowd by asking various persons to "move along" and to "stand back." Several members of the crowd accused the police officers of having no respect for "men of the cloth." They also made remarks to the effect that the police were always picking on the colored people for no reason at all. At first, only one or two members of the crowd made such remarks, but slowly more and more persons became involved.

HUDDLE QUESTIONS FOR "CROWD"—"INITIAL ENTRY"

Group A: What might have caused the crowd to become hostile toward the police officers? How could the police officers have avoided arousing the hostility of the crowd? How should a police officer handle an antagonistic and belligerent crowd?

Group B: The crowd accused the police officers of always picking on colored people, regardless of what they do. Why do you think they felt this way? Is there any justification to that accusation?

Discussion Points for "Crowd"—"Initial Entry"

Attitudes	Knowledges	Skills
A tolerance for the religious beliefs of others	Why some people feel abused or "picked on" by the police	Behaving so that the antagonism of the crowd is not aroused
How a person's "present mood" determines how he will react to others	The sense of values that people possess	Determining the hostility level of a crowd
Why police officers take out their personal gripes on the public	The cultures of minority groups	Ignoring a crowd's behavior
	The religious beliefs of others	Dispersing a crowd
	Ethics and professionalism in police work	Verbally abusing a person
	Prejudice, its nature and derivation	Explaining the law to people
	The civil rights laws	Explaining the constitutional rights to a citizen
		Taking into consideration that some people are not aware that they have violated the law before deciding upon what action to take toward them
		Making quick decisions on a course of action to follow
		Taking actions you think your supervisors would want you to take

LEAD QUESTIONS FOR "CROWD"—"INITIAL ENTRY"

1. Did Officer Morgan display religious intolerance? Was he justified or unjustified? Why?
2. How could a greater understanding of the cultural patterns of minority groups lead to more harmonious intergroup relationships?
3. Mental homogeneity, emotionality, and irrationality are said to characterize crowd behavior. What are these and how do they act?

CASE V—CROWD
STAGE 2—DATA EVALUATION
Group Material

The crowd's size slowly grew. In an effort to disperse the crowd, Officer Morgan threatened to "pull in everyone" if the various crowd members did not "move along." With this, the crowd became more antagonistic, jeered more loudly, dared the police officers to arrest them, and exclaimed that the police couldn't make an arrest because no one had committed a wrong. Morgan, who at this point was beginning to lose his temper, told the nearest crowd members to "get the hell away." He took his night stick and swung at their legs, forcing them to move back.

The religious solicitors remained silent during this action. They neither denied their guilt nor acclaimed their innocence.

**HUDDLE QUESTIONS FOR "CROWD"—
"DATA EVALUATION"**

Group A: List those actions of the officers which were incorrect. What, if anything, might the officers have done or said to present a better picture of themselves? What should the officers do now? What, in this case, might be the effect of an arrest?

Group B: In many cases, racial prejudice involves a passive avoidance of the minority group by the prejudiced person or in the withdrawal of certain privileges from members of the minority group. Do you think the

Discussion Points for "Crowd" — "Data Evaluation"

Attitudes	Knowledges	Skills
Why crowds may verbally abuse an officer	Why crowds may not cooperate with an officer's request	Behaving so that the antagonism of a crowd is not aroused
How a person's "present mood" will determine how he will react to others	Why some people may feel abused or "picked on" by the police	Explaining to a crowd the reasons for your actions
Why police officers take out their personal gripes on the public	The way certain people think	Determining the hostility level of a crowd
	The cultures of minority groups	Ignoring a crowd's behavior
	The dynamics of human personality	Explaining the law to people
	What factors contribute to the antagonism of a crowd	Determining whether or not a person is telling the truth
	The reasons why a crowd may not agree with police actions	Deciding why a person may be lying
	The civil rights laws	Deciding whether or not a crime has been committed
		Considering all complications that might arise if you decided to make an arrest

police officers, in any way, might have led the crowd members to feel like "second class" citizens?

LEAD QUESTIONS FOR "CROWD"—"DATA EVALUATION"

1. Why do crowd members refuse a police officer's request to disperse? What are the best and most effective ways to disperse crowds?
2. Do you think that the police had sufficient reason to arrest either the religious solicitors or any other crowd members? What evidence would you offer to support your conclusions?
3. Would the crowd have been equally hostile and antagonistic if the men in question were not religious leaders?
4. Why do you think the crowd jeered the police officers?
5. Why will people, as members of a crowd, perform acts which they would ordinarily avoid?
6. "Synthetic heat" has been said to weld crowd behavior. Did the officers create any "synthetic heat" in this instance?

CASE V—CROWD
STAGE 3—CONSUMMATING THE PLAN

Group Material

While the officers, still standing with the religious solicitors, were discussing an appropriate course of action, the two "sisters" came out of the building. Having been partially satisfied by the appearance of the "sisters," the police officers decided not to make an arrest. They advised the group to obtain a permit before they solicited again. The religious leader apologized to the police officers for this misunderstanding and assured them that it wouldn't happen again. As the police officers left, the crowd began to disperse slowly.

HUDDLE QUESTIONS FOR "CROWD"— "CONSUMMATING THE PLAN"

Group A: Do you think that the decision the police officers arrived at was the right one in this case? Why?

Group B: What factors welded the crowd in the first place? How did "imitation" and "contagion" contribute?

DISCUSSION FOR "CROWD"—"CONSUMMATING THE PLAN"

Attitudes	Knowledges	Skills	Decisions
How a person's "present mood" determines how he will react to others	The type of action you think your supervisors would want you to take	Ignoring a crowd's behavior	To book or not to book someone
Why police officers take out their personal gripes on the public	The civil rights laws	Determining the hostility level of a crowd	That sufficient and legitimate cause for police action does or does not exist
	Ethics and professionalism in police work	Making quick decisions on a course of action to follow	To caution someone about his actions
	How to pacify a crowd	Deciding whether or not a crime has been committed	To move and disperse crowds
	Why crowds may not agree with your actions	Treating more educated people differently than less educated people	To offer advice
	The sense of values that people possess	Behaving so that the antagonism of the crowd is not aroused	To obtain information of a non routine nature
		Explaining to the crowd the reasons for your actions	That a person was or was not telling the truth
		Dispersing a crowd	To show authority or to threaten with intent to impress or frighten

What similarities exist between this behavior and the crowd which forms when someone shouts, "Look, there's Elvis Presley?" What additional advice could the police officers have offered the religious solicitors?

LEAD QUESTIONS FOR "CROWD"— "CONSUMMATING THE PLAN"

1. Were the police officers correct in trying to disperse the crowd? What are some of the dangers inherent in crowd formations?
2. Would the officers have been equally correct in trying to disperse the crowd if it was not antagonistic and unruly or would they have been better advised to ignore it?
3. How would your supervisors want such a case handled?

CASE VI—ARGUMENTATIVE NEIGHBORS STAGE 1—INITIAL ENTRY

Group Material

Police Officers Jordan and Robinson were notified, while riding in their squad car, that two neighbors were arguing on the street. It was 8:30 p.m. on a warm Friday evening. Several minutes after receiving the message, they arrived on the scene.

The neighbors had been arguing in front of their homes for fifteen to twenty minutes. The neighborhood involved, a semi-suburban residential section, is composed primarily of single homes. The residents of the neighborhood are mostly Catholic, although there are Protestant and Jewish families scattered throughout.

The officers approached the two men, and Officer Jordan asked, "Okay, what seems to be the trouble?" Mr. Craig, one of the arguing neighbors, in a very animated, excited manner told the police that his neighbor, Mr. Solomon, ". . . is always parking his car in front of my house when he has plenty of space in front of his. I asked him to move his car and he won't budge."

Officer Jordan turned toward Mr. Solomon in order to give him an opportunity to offer an explanation. Mr. Solomon had difficulty expressing himself fluently in English. Speaking with a heavy, European accent, he told Officer Jordan, "Officer, when I came home from work this afternoon, there were two cars parked in front of my house and I had to park here." He went on to say, "This man has been making my life miserable ever since I moved here a year and a half ago. He lets his dog mess on my lawn, he sits outside late at night and puts the ball game on the radio full blast so I can't go to sleep. When I ask him not to do these things, he makes nasty remarks. Why should he do these things to me? I never bothered him. I pay taxes just like he does."

At this point, Mr. Craig, turning to Mr. Solomon, exclaimed, "You Jews are all alike. Hitler didn't take care of enough of you. We didn't have any trouble before you Jews moved here." Officer Robinson, in a firm, castigating voice, said, "You just watch what the hell you say. His being Jewish has nothing to do with this."

HUDDLE QUESTIONS FOR "ARGUMENTATIVE NEIGHBORS"—"INITIAL ENTRY"

Group A: Fundamentally, Mr. Craig was right. We know that all Jews are shrewd, clever, mercenary and just a little bit different. If they move into a neighborhood, they try to change it and just don't fit in. Discuss and critically evaluate these statements.

Group B: All ethnic groups possess basic, lasting and unmodifiable traits which make them different from other groups. Discuss and critically evaluate this statement.

LEAD QUESTIONS FOR "ARGUMENTATIVE NEIGHBORS"—"INITIAL ENTRY"

1. What are some of the reasons for the development of anti-Semitism among non-Jews?
2. How do you think Officer Robinson's comment could affect the situation? How would you feel if you were Mr. Craig?
3. Would you have explained to Mr. Craig the ill effects of his anti-Jewish attitudes upon his community? What might have been said?

DISCUSSION POINTS FOR "ARGUMENTATIVE NEIGHBORS" — "INITIAL ENTRY"

Attitudes	Knowledges	Skills
How a person's "present mood" determines how he will react to others	The way certain people think	Explaining the law to people
	The sense of values that people possess	Trying to pacify a person
	The causes for racial tension in mixed neighborhoods	Answering coherent questions politely
	Methods used to reduce tension in mixed neighborhoods	Explaining the constitutional rights to a citizen
	The civil rights laws	Explaining to people the ill effects their behavior has upon the community in which they reside
	Prejudice, its nature and derivation	Making quick decisions on a course of action to follow
	Ethics and professionalism in police work	Taking actions that you think your supervisors would want you to take

4. Do Jews "control" this country through their money lending activities?
5. What do you think of this "joke"? Currently, this country is owned by Jews, run by the Catholics on the basis of the vote of the Protestants, for the benefit of the Negroes? How true is the "joke"?

CASE VI—ARGUMENTATIVE NEIGHBORS
STAGE 2—DATA EVALUATION

Group Material

Officer Robinson turned to Mr. Solomon and asked, "Since the cars that were parked in front of your house have been moved, why don't you pull up? Try to park in front of your house whenever you can so that you don't have to annoy your neighbor." Mr. Solomon replied, "Officer, I can't drive the car; it's the Sabbath and I'm not allowed to."

Officer Jordan became a little annoyed at Mr. Solomon's unwillingness to cooperate and said, "What do you mean you can't drive because of the Sabbath?" Mr. Solomon explained that members of his religion celebrate the Sabbath from sunset on Friday to sunset on Saturday. He pointed to his neighbor and continued, "I tried to explain this to him but he won't listen."

Mr. Craig interrupted at this point and said, "Naturally, I won't listen to him. Ever since I was a kid in school, I realized that all Jews are conniving. Whenever they don't want to do something, they make up excuses. He's not telling the truth—I've even seen a Jewish Rabbi drive on Saturday. Don't believe him, Officer."

Officer Jordan asked Mr. Solomon if Mr. Craig's statement was true. Mr. Solomon explained that not all Jews are orthodox and those who are not do not observe some rules. But since he was orthodox, he could not drive his car on the Sabbath. Officer Jordan, in a moment of despair, turned to Officer Robinson and said, "Well, what do we do?"

HUDDLE QUESTIONS FOR "ARGUMENTATIVE NEIGHBORS"—"DATA EVALUATION"

Group A: Why is it important to understand the religious beliefs

Discussion Points for "Argumentative Neighbors"—"Data Evaluation"		
Attitudes	*Knowledges*	*Skills*
How a person's "present mood" determines how he will react to others	The way certain people think	Being polite to people when interrogating them
Why officers take out their personal gripes on the public	The sense of values that people possess	Trying to pacify a person
Why neighbors argue	A person's point of view on a given issue	Determining the feelings of a community with regard to racial, religious, or national origin tension after an incident has occurred
	The cultures of minority groups	
	The dynamics of personality	Getting all the facts from the people concerned at the scene of an incident
	Ethics and professionalism in police work	Explaining the constitutional rights to a citizen
	Why officers should not take sides in a dispute between neighbors	Deciding whether or not a crime has been committed
	The causes for racial tension in a neighborhood	Understanding that all members of minority groups are neither all good nor all bad
	Prejudice, its nature and derivation	
	The religious beliefs of others	

of others? If there were a more thorough understanding of the religious beliefs of others, how might it have changed the course of the argument?

Group B: Social scientists are agreed that prejudices are learned and not inborn or inherited. Research studies have shown that prejudice is rarely, if ever, displayed in children before the ages of three or four. In light of this, what suggestions would you make to help overcome discrimination against Jews? How would you handle the problem with adults who may already be predisposed to anti-Semitism?

LEAD QUESTIONS FOR "ARGUMENTATIVE NEIGHBORS"—"DATA EVALUATION"

1. Discuss and evaluate:

  (a)   Physical differences among ethnic groups indicate the inherent superiority or inferiority of certain groups.
  (b)   Those who give service are inferior to those who plan or are served.
  (c)   The total number of an ethnic group that are professionals, such as doctors or lawyers, represents a criterion against which the cultural advancement of the group can be measured.

2. What can the officers do?
3. How do you think the police officers could be more effective in trying to help the neighbors amicably solve their differences?
4. Did the police have adequate information on which to base their forthcoming decisions? What additional information would you have tried to obtain before you tried to solve the problem?

CASE VI—ARGUMENTATIVE NEIGHBORS
STAGE 3—DECISION MAKING

Group Material

Officer Robinson suggested to Mr. Solomon, "Why don't you give your car key to Mr. Craig and he will drive your car up to

DISCUSSION POINTS FOR "ARGUMENTATIVE NEIGHBORS"—"DECISION MAKING"

Attitudes	Knowledges	Skills	Decisions
How a person's "present mood" determines how he will react to others	Why some people may feel abused or "picked on" by the police	Making quick decisions on a course of action to follow	To caution someone about his actions
Why officers take out their personal gripes on the public	The way people think	Pacifying hostile neighbors	To offer advice
	A person's point of view on a given issue	Explaining to belligerent neighbors why their behavior is objectionable	That the person was or was not telling the truth
	The cultures of minority groups	Trying to reduce tension in a mixed neighborhood	
	Ethics and professionalism in police work		

the house?" Mr. Solomon obligingly handed the key to Mr. Craig. Mr. Craig parked the car in front of the Solomon residence and handed the key to Officer Robinson who, in turn, gave it to Mr. Solomon.

Officer Jordan then said to the two neighbors, "If you two tried to understand each other better instead of jumping to conclusions and getting hot headed over little things, you'd be much better off."

Neither Mr. Craig nor Mr. Solomon said anything. Each walked to his home as the officers drove away.

HUDDLE QUESTIONS FOR "ARGUMENTATIVE NEIGHBORS"—"DECISION MAKING"

Group A: Did the officers come to the right conclusions in trying to settle the argument? What would you have done? What additional advice would you have offered the argumentative neighbors?

Group B: Do you think that Mr. Solomon was completely satisfied with the way the police handled the situation? Mr. Craig? How are the two neighbors likely to get along in the future?

LEAD QUESTIONS FOR "ARGUMENTATIVE NEIGHBORS"—"DECISION MAKING"

1. On the basis of the information obtained, do you think Officer Jordan should have been more direct with the neighbors and cautioned them against certain of their actions?
2. What, if anything, would you have cautioned Mr. Craig against? What, if anything, would you have cautioned Mr. Solomon against?
3. Should the officers have explained to the belligerent neighbors why their behavior is objectionable? Why?
4. Why do you think the officers did not try to help the neighbors resolve their differences?

CASE VII—FIGHTS AND RIOTS
STAGE 1—INITIAL ENTRY

Group Material

James Rodriguez, age 28, a Puerto Rican living in this country for the past three years, was driving from his home to his job as a construction laborer on a hot, muggy, June morning. At 6:30 a.m., he was driving on Huntingdon Street, which is in a heavily populated Negro neighborhood. He noticed two white men walking in the road. They were staggering and leaning against each other.

As Rodriquez approached the corner, he stopped for a red light. While waiting for the light to change, he heard the two men singing and screaming at the top of their lungs. Rodriguez stared at the men. One of the men on the street noticed Rodriguez watching them and yelled, "What's the matter, Spic? Don't you like it?"

Rodriguez, turning to watch for the light to turn green, realized that the men were approaching his car. He didn't have time to roll up his windows so he locked his left side door. One of the men practically leaped through the window and started to swing at him. Rodriguez was trying to push the man out of the car when the attacker yelled, "This fuckin' Spic put his hand in my face. I won't let no Spic put his hand in my face." With this, he became more violent, and continued to swing and punch Rodriguez. Rodriguez moved out of the driver's seat to the opposite side of the car. The other man and a third party (who had subsequently joined these two) opened the right side door, which was not locked, and dragged Rodriguez out of the car.

As Rodriguez was being dragged from his car, he reached down to the floor, where he kept various tools, and picked up a pipe. He managed to break loose from the men, started swinging the pipe, and warned the three men to keep away from him. The three men charged at him and a fight ensued.

Rodriguez yelled to the crowd which had formed, "Help me! Don't let those fellows kill me—they're drunk!" No one from the crowd, which was mainly made up of Negroes, came to his assistance. He finally managed to break loose and rolled over on top of one of the men. While pinning the man to the ground, Rodriguez reached into his pocket, pulled out a knife, and put it to his attacker's throat. Rodriguez called to the other two men, "If you don't stop fighting me, I'm going to slit his throat." A short while later, Rodriguez noticed a police officer, with gun in hand, breaking through the crowd.

As the police officer approached the fight, a Negro bystander stopped him and said, "These men are drunk, Officer. I saw them attack this fellow" (pointing to Rodriguez). The police officer ignored the man and continued on to separate the two fighting men. The officer then took the knife from Rodriguez. The man who was pinned to the ground by Rodriguez jumped to his feet and started to swing at Rodriguez. The police officer pushed him aside saying, "Come on, buddy. Take it easy." The man then begin swinging at the officer yelling, "Get your fuckin' hands off me! I'm goin' to kill that Spic!"

At the same time, two other police officers (who in the meantime had broken through the crowd to the scene of the fight) jumped on this man and handcuffed him. The first police officer grabbed Rodriguez and said to the man, "Don't worry about this Spic. We'll take care of him."

At this point, Rodriguez, in an animated tone, blurted out several sentences in Spanish. The police officer replied, "Speak English. Speak English." Rodriguez belligerently replied, "Sure go on. Blame it all on me. It's all my fault. You cops don't give us people a break." With this, he spit on the officer. The officer then punched Rodriguez in the face and handcuffed him.

HUDDLE QUESTIONS FOR "FIGHTS AND RIOTS"— "INITIAL ENTRY"

Group A: Do you think that Rodriguez, as a member of a minority group, felt abused or discriminated against by the police officer? Were these feelings justified or was he being oversensitive? How would you describe his attitude toward the police officer? Why might Rodriguez have developed this attitude? How would you interpret his spitting on the officer and what does it signify? Is this a pattern peculiar to Puerto Ricans or is it common to other peoples under certain situations?

Group B: It has been said that frustrations (blocks) of certain needs often find expression in aggressive acts which may ease the frustrated state. How might this statement apply to the three men who attacked Rodriguez? How does one acquire racial prejudice? What factors (cultural and psychological) cause people to maintain their attitudes once they are acquired?

LEAD QUESTIONS FOR "FIGHTS AND RIOTS"— "INITIAL ENTRY"

1. Do you think that any of the police officers displayed racial prejudice in this case? If so, how? Do you think that the crowd would feel that any of the officers prejudged the guilt of the parties involved or would they appear impartial? Justify your response.
2. What actions of police officers cause members of minority groups to conclude that they are not being treated fairly? What might police officers do to make members of minority groups feel that they are being treated fairly?
3. Criticize the police officer's approach in this case. How would you have handled it?
4. How should you react and what might have been said to Rodriguez when he started to speak Spanish? Was the police officer justified in hitting Rodriguez? Why do you think the police officer responded in this fashion?
5. What reasons can you offer for the fact that none of the Negro bystanders came to Rodriguez's defense? To the defense of the white man whom Rodriguez had threatened to kill?

DISCUSSION POINTS FOR "FIGHTS AND RIOTS"—"INITIAL ENTRY"

Attitudes	Knowledges	Skills
How a person's "present mood" determines how he will react to people	Not all members of minority groups are either all good or all bad	Preventing fights
Why officers take out their personal gripes on the public	Why people feel abused or "picked on" by the police	Breaking up fights
	Why some people possess an arrogant attitude toward the police	Rescuing a person from physical punishment inflicted upon him by a group
	The ways in which certain people think	Disarming adults of their weapons
	The sense of values that certain people possess	Tolerating verbal abuse
	The cultural patterns of certain minority groups	Verbally abusing a person
	The unique slang used by certain groups	Employing the unique slang used by people when talking with them
	The causes for racial tension	Determining the severity of a person's injury
	What methods are used to reduce racial tension	Making quick decisions on a course of action to follow
	The civil rights laws	Taking action that you think your supervisors would want you to take
		Explaining the law to people
		Trying to pacify a person

Discussion Points for "Fights and Riots"—"Initial Entry" (Continued)

Knowledges	*Skills*
Prejudice, its nature and derivation	Explaining to people the ill effects their behavior has upon the community in which they reside
Ethics and professionalism in police work	Being polite to people when interrogating them
	Trying to pacify a person
	Determining whether or not an incident between whites and non-whites was caused by racial differences
	Determining the feelings of a community with regard to racial, religious, or national origin tension after an incident has occurred
	Getting all the facts from people concerned at the scene of an incident
	Explaining the constitutional rights to a citizen

CASE VII—FIGHTS AND RIOTS
STAGE 2—DECISION MAKING

Group Material

As the three men and Rodriguez, all handcuffed, were being led to the wagon, Rodriguez again started yelling in Spanish. The police officer told Rodriguez to keep quiet. Rodriguez ignored the officer and continued yelling in Spanish. The police officer pushed Rodriguez, who fell against the wagon and hit his head. Rodriguez, who was dazed, started to stagger. He was caught by another officer, who said, "Where do you think you're going?" The officer punched Rodriguez.

The Negro spectator, who had tried to tell the first officer the details of the fight, approached another officer to tell the officer about the incident. The first officer grabbed the Negro and said, "Let's throw him in, too; he was in it. Something ought to be done to keep these damn troublemakers in their places."

Several Negro women started to protest as the police put the Negro man in the wagon along with Rodriguez and the three men. The women yelled that the Negro was innocent and had nothing to do with the fight. The police officers tried to break up the crowd, which had now moved to the wagon. Ignoring the protesting women, the officer said, "O.K., the fight's over. Go on home. Let's break it up."

HUDDLE QUESTIONS FOR "FIGHTS AND RIOTS"— "DECISION MAKING"

Group A: Stereotypy is defined as a widespread belief or tendency regarding an entire group of people. An example might be the notation that Negroes are carefree and happy-go-lucky. Were the police officers guilty of stereotyping Negroes? If so, how? Were they guilty of stereotyping Puerto Ricans? If so, how? Why are stereotyped concepts of minority groups detrimental to harmonious integration among people? How would you go about combatting the detrimental stereotype that many people have about Negroes and Puerto Ricans and replace them with more realistic and dynamic understandings of minority groups?

Group B: Were the police officers ethical and professional in their handling of the situation? What might the effect on the crowd be relative to the police officers' treatment of the Negro man? Were the police justified in this treatment? What would you have done in this situation? Should police officers be concerned with the complications that might arise from this type of arrest or should their primary concern be to break up the fight and arrest those involved? Why?

LEAD QUESTIONS FOR "FIGHTS AND RIOTS"— "DECISION MAKING"

1. How might the behavior of the police officers affect the attitudes and behavior of other younger and less experienced police officers who might have been assigned to this case?
2. How would you have felt if you were the Negro man? What would you have done in this situation?
3. What might the reactions of police supervisors be if the details of the case were presented to them?
4. What would you have done if you were a witness to this incident?
5. Where do you think the police officers made their biggest single mistake and how would you have handled it?

Discussion Points for "Fights and Riots"—"Decision Making"

Attitudes	Knowledges	Skills	Decisions
How a person's "present mood" determines how he will react to people	The ways in which certain people think	Taking into consideration the causes for a fight before taking final action	When to book a person
Why officers take out their personal gripes on the public	The cultural patterns of minority groups	Determining whether a person is telling the truth	That sufficient and legitimate cause for police action does or does not exist
Why people verbally abuse an officer	The unique slang used by people	Deciding why a person may be lying	Cautioning someone about his actions
	The dynamics of personality	Determining whether an incident between whites and non-whites was caused by racial differences	Moving and dispersing crowds
	The civil rights laws		When to offer advice
	Ethics and professionalism in police work	Determining the feelings of a community with regard to racial, religious, or national origin tension after an incident has occurred	When to obtain information (under what circumstances) of a non-routine nature
	Why some people feel abused or "picked on" by the police		When to show authority or threaten with intent to impress or frighten
	People's points of view on a given issue	Determining the severity of a person's injury	To break up a fight
	The causes of racial tension	Deciding whether a crime has been committed	Determining if a person was connected with an incident
	The causes for community tension		When to strike someone
	Prejudice, its nature and derivation		

Discussion Points for "Fights and Riots" — "Decision Making" (Continued)

Knowledges	*Skills*	*Decisions*
The methods used to reduce racial tension	Considering all possible complications that might arise if you decided to make an arrest	When to ignore an offender's excuse for a misdemeanor
The types of actions your supervisors would want you to take	Being firm with people and not granting them any special favors despite their background hardships	When to refuse a person's request
All members of minority groups are neither good nor bad	Making quick decisions on a course of action to follow	
	Treating more educated people differently than less educated people	

CASE VII—FIGHTS AND RIOTS
STAGE 3—CONSUMMATING THE PLAN

Group Material

While the wagon was being driven away, Rodriguez, in broken English, and with a pronounced Spanish accent, tried to tell the officers of the incident. One of the officers said, "Save it 'till later, boy. You'll have a lot of explainin' to do." Another police officer then grabbed Rodriguez, threw him face down on the floor of the wagon, and placed the sole of his foot on the back of Rodriguez' neck to keep him from squirming.

Rodriguez, whose clothes were heavily saturated with blood, and who suffered a broken nose, broken leg, and many cuts and abrasions as a result of the fight and the police beating was taken to the station house, booked and locked in a cell. After several hours in the cell, other police officers washed the blood from Rodriguez' body with a water hose and took him to a hospital, where he remained for three weeks.

All five men were held for court. The charges were: aggravated assault and battery, assault with a deadly weapon, and assault and battery with intent to kill.

HUDDLE QUESTIONS FOR "FIGHTS AND RIOTS"— "CONSUMMATING THE PLAN"

Group A: If you were Rodriguez, what would you have done in an attempt to clear your name? Would you take the case to any of the community human relations agencies? If so, why? If not, why? How do community human relations agencies help to achieve harmonious relations between the police and public?

Group B: Theorists have claimed that two of the most effective methods of propagating racial prejudice are through "direct" training (e.g., teaching children to stay away from Negroes because "they are dirty and foul mouthed") and "indirect" training (e.g., overhearing comments such as "Jim, the porter, probably uses all his money to get drunk—like all colored people"). Do you think that people become prejudiced against

Discussion Points for "Fights and Riots"—"Consummating the Plan"

Attitudes	Knowledges	Skills
How a person's "present mood" determines how he will react to people	Why people attack officers	Breaking up fights
Why officers take out their personal gripes on the public	The cultural pattern of minority groups	Utilizing your knowledges of the causes of a fight to terminate it
	The causes of racial tension	Disarming adults of their weapons
	Ethics and professionalism in police work	Verbally abusing a person
		Arresting a person for disorderly conduct (loud and/or obscene language)
		Explaining the law to people
		Trying to pacify a person
		Taking actions you think your supervisors would want you to take
		Trying to reduce racial tension in a mixed neighborhood
		Being firm with people and not granting them any special favors despite their background hardships

members of minority groups through one or both forms of training? Through what other means could racial prejudice develop? What actions would you take to halt prejudice in light of these methods?

LEAD QUESTIONS FOR "FIGHTS AND RIOTS"— "CONSUMMATING THE PLAN"

1. Why is it important for police officers to understand the problems of minority groups? In what ways will this help them to serve these citizens better?
2. Why has the influx of Puerto Ricans to the mainland been so prevalent in recent years? Why might Puerto Ricans see a city as friendly? As an unfriendly city?
3. Why might in-migrant groups see police as an accepting group? As a rejecting group? What might be the effect on the attitudes of members of minority groups when they perceive that they are accepted by other minority groups and the majority groups? When they perceive that they are rejected by other minority and majority groups?
5. Why is it important that minority groups see police officers as friendly towards them?

CASE VIII—BURGLARY INVESTIGATION ROLE PLAY INSTRUCTIONS

Conference Leader Instructions

Procedure

1. Read the *Introduction and Background* to the group.
2. Ask for volunteers for the roles of
   a. Police Officer Burke
   b. Police Officer Rice
   c. The Negro woman

The role players need not be members of the same race or sex as called for by the case material. If no one volunteers for the roles, select three people.

3. Allow each player to read only the instructions for his own role. Do not pass the role material to the rest of the group. Allow the players enough time to read and understand their roles.

4. Provide the needed props. In the first stage, only two chairs, two pads, and two pencils are necessary. Place the chairs side by side. They represent the front seat of the patrol car in which Officers Burke and Rice are seated when the incident starts. The pads and pencils are for Officers Burke and Rice.

5. When the players are ready, ask them to take their places. The police officers are seated. The Negro lady is off to the side and comes running toward the police officers.

6. There is no specified time limit, but stop each stage after fifteen minutes if the role playing extends that long.

7. After the role playing for this stage has terminated, give the players their role material for the second stage and read the *Introduction* to that stage to the group. For the second stage, supply the players with a table and three chairs. Place the table, with the chairs around it, slightly off to one side. Tell the players that the table and chairs represent the kitchen of the woman's apartment. Place a milk bottle, filled with water, in a corner of the table. After the second stage has terminated, repeat the process for the last stage.

8. When the last stage is finished, conduct the discussion with the entire group. There will be no "huddles." During the discussion be sure to allow the actors to save face by stating their reactions and why they responded as they did.

CASE VIII—BURGLARY INVESTIGATION
STAGE 1—INITIAL ENTRY

Introduction and Background

Police Officers Burke and Rice (both white) were on patrol when they noticed a young Negro woman waving to them from the side of the road. She was wearing only a light sweater on a cold, cloudy January afternoon. The woman appeared highly agitated. As the officers stopped their car, the woman shouted that her apartment had just been robbed.

The neighborhood in which the burglary occurred is almost entirely Negro. It is a very low income area. The houses, in many instances, are very old and in poor repair. The crime rate is high; there have been many burglaries reported in the past.

DISCUSSION POINTS FOR "BURGLARY INVESTIGATION"—"INITIAL ENTRY"

Attitudes	*Knowledges*	*Skills*
How a person's "present mood" determines how he will react to other people	The unique slang used by people	Employing the unique slang used by people when talking with them
Why officers take out their personal gripes on the public	The civil rights laws	Tolerating verbal abuse
	Ethics and professionalism in police work	Verbally abusing a person
		Trying to pacify a person
		Answering coherent questions
		Explaining the constitutional rights to a citizen
		Making quick decisions on a course of action to follow
		Taking action that you think your supervisors would want you to take

Roles of Officers Burke and Rice

Conduct your total initial investigation in the street in your patrol car. This incident occurs early in the evening shortly after the start of your shift. You have plenty of time. Tend to be thorough but abrupt.

Ask all the questions necessary for a complete initial investigation as well as questions such as "Don't you lock your belongings up if you leave the house?" "Who are your neighbors, honey?" "Are you married?" "How old are you?" "Is this the only thing you do to make money?" etc.

Role of Negro Woman

You are a widow in your late twenties and rent three rooms in your apartment to four single persons. This is your source of income. This afternoon one of the boarders moved out of your apartment to go to New York and look for work. The boarder had recently moved to this city and was unable to find steady employment. You left your apartment to go shopping around 3:00 p.m. When you returned about 5:30 p.m., you started to clean the apartment. You noticed that your winter coat, several dresses and your jewelry were missing.

You assume that this boarder was the thief. Run towards the police officers, who are in their patrol car, and tell them that you were just robbed. You are very excited and speak very rapidly. Beg the police officers to find the thief.

Show that you are anxious for quick service. Show that you think that the police are wasting too much time by standing in the street asking all those "silly" questions. Make remarks such as, "Those questions aren't necessary. I told you the thief is the boarder." "I should think that you would be better off contacting the bus station. That crook may still be there. Why waste time sitting in your car?" And "What difference does it make? Your job is to catch the thief—not to prosecute me." Be very critical of the way they handle the case. Don't be afraid to let them know you think they are wasting time.

Try to play this role as you think a young Negro woman might; be realistic. Think back to your experience in which there was a similar situation.

CASE VIII—BURGLARY INVESTIGATION
STAGE 2—FACT FINDING

Introduction

After obtaining the preliminary information from the Negro woman, Officers Burke and Rice decided to enter the apartment for further investigation. They accompanied the complainant to her apartment. The apartment was on the top floor of a dark, dingy house. The rooms were very small and poorly furnished. The total apartment consisted of a kitchen, bathroom, three bedrooms (which were rented to boarders), and another room which was furnished as a combination bedroom-living room. All the boarders were out.

Roles of Officers Burke and Rice

Take the woman to her apartment; ask to be shown around the apartment. Perform a search in each room. Ask any and all required questions. If she says anything which makes you believe that more may be going on in the apartment than meets the eye, probe in order to get complete details. The lady will lead to you to the kitchen, where your investigation of the burglary and of anything else that makes you suspicious may be continued.

Role of Negro Woman

You are still annoyed with the police officers and think they are wasting too much time. Tell them that if they want to catch the thief, they should hurry and not detain you by asking all these "silly" questions. Take them into the apartment if they want to look around but tell them that it isn't necessary for them to search because you did so before you ran down to get them.

Eventually, lead the officers to the kitchen, where they will continue their interrogation. When you get to the kitchen, you realize that by being so critical with the officers, you may have offended them and that this may cause them to do less than a thorough job. Try to rectify this by being more polite and hospitable. Offer them a drink of whiskey because it's so cold outside. The whiskey is in the milk bottle on the table.

DISCUSSION POINTS FOR "BURGLARY INVESTIGATION"—"FACT FINDING"

Attitudes	*Knowledges*	*Skills*
How a person's "present mood" determines how he will react to people	The unique slang used by people	Employing the unique slang used by people when talking with them
Why officers take out their personal gripes on the public	The dynamics of human personality	Obtaining information from the victims of a burglary in a polite manner
	The civil rights laws	Looking for clues without damaging personal property or injuring personal feelings
	Ethics and professionalism in police work	Making a victim feel that you will do everything possible to apprehend an offender and recover stolen property
		Being polite to people when interrogating them
		Being patient when interrogating people
		Explaining the law to people
		Getting all the facts from people concerned involved in the incident
		Taking into consideration the fact that some people are not aware that they violated the law before deciding upon what action to take toward them
		Being firm with people and not granting them any special favor despite their background hardships

CASE VIII—BURGLARY INVESTIGATION
STAGE 3—DECISION MAKING

Roles of Officers Burke and Rice

On the basis of the information you have obtained, make the appropriate decision and close the event.

Role of Negro Woman

You are still a little leary about the effectiveness and adequacy with which the police officers are handling your case. Continue pressing for quick and adequate police service.

LEAD QUESTIONS FOR "BURGLARY INVESTIGATION"— "INITIAL ENTRY"

1. What actions on the part of the officers might have been interpreted by the Negro woman as showing a lack of police interest in her specific case? A lack of politeness?
2. In what ways did the officers show evidence of poor or ineffective social behaviors?
3. What effective or agreeable social behaviors did the officers demonstrate? Why?
4. What, if any, modification of behavior would be called for on the part of the officers if the complainant had been a young Negro man? A white woman?
5. Why might a woman take in boarders without adequate reference checks?
6. Why might the officers have been abrupt with the Negro woman? What in their immediate past might have led to this behavior? What in their distant past might have led to this behavior?

LEAD QUESTIONS FOR "BURGLARY INVESTIGATION"— "FACT FINDING"

1. Do you think the officers displayed adequate sympathy and understanding of the woman's problem? How might they have been more effective in making her feel that they would do everything possible to apprehend the thief?
2. What would your reactions be if you were the Negro woman

DISCUSSION POINTS FOR "BURGLARY INVESTIGATION"—"DECISION MAKING"

Attitudes	Knowledges	Skills	Decisions
How a person's "present mood" determines how he will react to other people	What actions would your supervisors want you to take	Making quick decisions on a course of action to follow	To book or not to book some-one
	The civil rights laws	Deciding whether or not a crime has been committed	That sufficient and legitimate cause for police action taken does or does not exist
	The dynamics of human personality	Treating more educated people differently than less educated people	To offer advice
	Prejudice, its nature and derivation	Determining whether or not the person is telling the truth	To obtain information of a non-routine nature
	Ethics and professionalism in police work	Taking into consideration that some people are not aware that they violated the law before deciding upon what action to take toward them	That the person was or was not telling the truth
		Deciding why a person may be lying	To joke with or humor some-one
		Being firm with people and not granting them any special favors despite their background hardships	To refuse a person's request

Discussion Points for "Burglary Investigation"—"Decision Making" (Continued)

Skills

Explaining to a person how to protect his property

Making a victim feel that the officer will do everything possible to apprehend an offender and recover stolen property

Explaining the law to people

Answering coherent questions politely

and the police officers ignored your requests not to search your apartment?

3. Do you think the woman was concealing any information from the officers? What clues led you to believe this?

4. Do you think the police handled the whiskey incident adequately? What would you have done in a similar situation? What types of behaviors were called for, on the part of the police officers, in questioning the woman about the whiskey?

5. What other pertinent information should the officers have acquired from the woman?

6. How did the officers display ethical behaviors in this case and in what ways were their behaviors unethical?

7. Would you have performed the same type of search as the officers? Criticize their methods and approach.

8. How would you interpret the changing of the woman's attitude toward the police officers?

LEAD QUESTIONS FOR "BURGLARY INVESTIGATION"— "DECISION MAKING"

1. Critically evaluate the decision made by the officers. What else could they have done?

2. Criticize the officers' exit from the apartment. What else could they have done or said before leaving the apartment? Why are these things important?

3. What, if any, advice could the officers have offered to the woman and why?

4. Were the police officers effective in trying to leave the woman in a better frame of mind than when they met her? Criticize their approach and tactics and elaborate on how you would go about trying to do this.

5. Why do you think the woman may have been dissatisfied with the way the police officers were handling the case?

6. Why is it important for police officers to gain the confidence of the citizens and convince them of their ability to do a good job? How might police officers go about improving police-public relations?

CASE IX—DRUNK
STAGE 1—FACT FINDING

Group Material

At 10:00 p.m. on January 20, Patrolman Becker, walking his beat in a neighborhood characterized by its slums, high density housing, low rentals, numerous bars, and large Negro population, noticed a Negro man staggering along the street. It was a cold, windy night and the streets were icy as a result of a heavy snow that had recently fallen. Becker suspected that the man was drunk. He politely approached the man and asked, "Are you feeling all right?" The man replied, "Go peddle your marbles someplace else." Becker, who could smell liquor on the man's breath, ignored this comment and told the drunk to go home because he could be "rolled" in his present condition. The officer reached out to grab hold of the drunk's arm as the drunk swayed from side to side. The drunk told him, "Get your mother fuckin' hands off me." Becker, ignoring this comment, said, "Come on, go home and go to bed." He watched as the drunk walked away.

HUDDLE QUESTIONS FOR "DRUNK"—"INITIAL ENTRY"

Group A: Was Patrolman Becker's approach in this incident proper? Is poor balance and the detection of liquor on one's breath sufficient for indicating intoxication? How would you determine if a person had been drinking to excess? Was Becker correct in ignoring the vile language the man was directing at him? Would you have ignored this verbal abuse or not? Why?

Group B: What are some of the reasons that the man involved may drink excessively? How can factors such as feelings of inferiority, uneasiness in social situations, escape from reality, and inwardly directed aggression play a part? Are these factors commonly found in people of all races and religions and from all walks of life?

DISCUSSION POINTS FOR "DRUNK"—"FACT FINDING"

Attitudes	*Knowledges*	*Skills*
How a person's "present mood" determines how he will react to other people	Why some people feel abused or "picked on" by the police	Determining whether a person has been drinking to excess
	Why some people possess arrogant attitudes toward the police	Tolerating verbal abuse
	The ways in which certain people think	Being polite to people when interrogating them
	The sense of values that people possess	Being patient when interrogating people
	The cutural pattern of certain minority groups	Explaining the law to people
	The unique slang used by certain groups	Making quick decisions on the course of action to follow
	Ethics and professionalism in police work	Taking action that you think your supervisors would want you to take
		Trying to pacify a person

LEAD QUESTIONS FOR "DRUNK"—"FACT FINDING"

1. Was the use of the term "rolled" a good choice of words for Patrolman Becker to use in trying to get his point across to the Negro man? Is it important for the police to know and be able to use the slang words used primarily by particular groups? Why? How important is it for police officers to "choose their words?"
2. Was it good judgment on Patrolman Becker's part to advise the man to ". . . go home and go to bed?" Should Becker have offered the man additional protection? What should be done if you see a man who appears to be drunk staggering down the street? Critically evaluate your point of view.
3. What are some of the effects of alcohol on behavior?
4. How might early childhood experiences lead to alcoholism in adulthood?
5. How true is it that people of some nationalities "like their liquor" more than people of other nationalities?

CASE IX—DRUNK
STAGE 2—DATA EVALUATION

Group Material

Officer Becker stood on the street and watched as the drunk walked away. However, instead of continuing on his way home, the drunk staggered toward a bar some fifty to sixty feet from where he was first accosted. The officer again approached the man and warned him that he would be arrested if he entered the bar. The drunk, at this point, started running away from the officer. As the man crossed the curb, he slipped on the ice, hit his head against a parked car as he fell, and started bleeding profusely. While the drunk (who was unconscious for several minutes) was lying on the ground, the officer asked a passerby to get a clean towel from the bar (so that he could wipe the blood from the drunk's head) and to call the station house for a wagon.

In short order, a crowd formed. Patrolman Becker thought it proper to explain the incident to one member of the crowd who asked, "What happened?"

Becker replied that he told the drunk to go home and that when the drunk started to enter the bar, he approached him again in order to tell him to go home. The crowd remained quiet and orderly.

HUDDLE QUESTIONS FOR "DRUNK"—"DATA EVALUATION"

Group A: Do you think there is any cultural basis for excessive drinking? Do you think that excessive drinking is more prevalent for certain ethnic groups than for others? Or do you feel that there are factors other than cultural which explain the reasons for excessive drinking? Defend your position.

Group B: Was Patrolman Becker correct in assuming it to be important to explain the incident to the crowd? Do you think that the crowd might have become aggressive if Becker had ignored them? Is it important to appease a crowd, even to the extent of lying? Why?

LEAD QUESTIONS FOR "DRUNK"—"DATA EVALUATION"

1. Was Patrolman Becker right in asking a passerby to get a towel and to call the station? Should he have perfomed these chores himself even if it meant leaving the scene of the incident?
2. Would you have applied first aid to the drunk? How would you go about determining the severity of the man's injury?
3. Do you think that the man was coherent enough to have answered certain questions that Patrolman Becker might have asked? Should Patrolman Becker have tried to learn why the man had been drinking excessively and why the man did not heed his advice?
4. Why do you think the drunk ran when Becker spoke to him at the entrance to the bar? Do you think that there was sufficient and legitimate cause for an arrest? Why? Would you have decided upon the same course of action as did Patrolman Becker? What might you have done which would have prevented the drunk from running away and consequently injuring himself?

DISCUSSION POINTS FOR "DRUNK"—"DATA EVALUATION"

Attitudes	Knowledges	Skills	Decisions
Why people drink to excess	Why some people feel abused or "picked on" by the police	Making quick decisions on a course of action to follow	When to book a person
How a person's "present mood" determines how he will react to other people	Why some people possess an arrogant attitude toward the police	Deciding whether a crime was committed	That sufficient and legitimate cause for police action does or does not exist
	The ways in which certain people think	Determining what action to take if a person has been drinking to excess	To caution someone about his actions
	The sense of values that people possess	Taking into consideration the reasons why a person may have been drinking to excess before deciding upon what action to take	Advising people about their actions
	The cultural patterns of certain minority groups		To show authority or to threaten with intent to impress or frighten
	Taking actions that you think your supervisors would want you to take	Determining the severity of a person's injury	Determining when medical attention is needed
	Ethics and professionalism in police work	Considering all possible complications that might arise if an arrest was decided upon	
	The dynamics of personality		
	All members of minority groups are neither good nor bad		

CASE IX—DRUNK
STAGE 3—CONSUMMATING THE PLAN

Group Material

The officer helped the drunk, who was now quiet, into the wagon. Becker explained to the man that he was being taken to the hospital where his wound would be treated and then he was going to be "locked up" for the night. The officer also pointed out the dangers of getting drunk and aimlessly walking the streets.

The following evening, Patrolman Becker saw the man walking down the street. The man was sober; he recognized the officer and greeted him in a friendly manner. There were no hard feelings on either person's part.

HUDDLE QUESTIONS FOR "DRUNK"— "CONSUMMATING THE PLAN"

Group A: Should Becker have assumed a sympathetic role toward the man or should he have been more authoritative and commanding? Which approach do you think would have been more effective? Why?

Group B: Why is it important for officers to act friendly and make friends on a beat? Do you think that Patrolman Becker, through his approach in this incident, could be effective in preventing this man from becoming drunk in public again? Should police officers be sympathetic toward drunks and regard them as sick individuals who need help, or should they, instead, view them as criminals who need punishment?

LEAD QUESTIONS FOR "DRUNK"— "CONSUMMATING THE PLAN"

1. Is there a greater incidence of drunkeness in slum areas than in higher income level neighborhoods? Why or why not?
2. Why might some drunks become hostile and belligerent while others become friendly and jovial?
3. Do you think that there is a relationship between intelligence and alcoholism?
4. Do you think that there is an innate basis for alcoholism?
5. How would you go about preventing alcoholism?

DISCUSSION POINTS FOR "DRUNK"—"CONSUMMATING THE PLAN"

Attitudes	Knowledges	Skills
How a person's "present mood" determines how he will react	Why some people feel abused or "picked on" by the police	Taking action toward a person who has been drinking to excess
	Why some people possess an arrogant attitude toward the police	Arresting a person for disorderly conduct (loud and/or obscene language)
	The cultural patterns of certain minority groups	Trying to pacify a person
	Ethics and professionalism in police work	Explaining to people the ill effects their behavior has upon the community in which they reside
		Employing the unique slang used by people when talking to them
		Taking action that you think your supervisors would want you to take
		Acknowledging friendly comments of people
		Making friends on the beat

CASE X—ARGUMENTATIVE MARRIED COUPLE
STAGE 1—FACT FINDING

Group Material

Officers Sheman and Young were answering a complaint phoned to police headquarters. Mrs. Tanner, who had placed the call, requested that police be sent to her apartment. She had been fighting with her husband, who had beaten and injured her.

On entering the downstairs hallway, the officers noticed a man. The officers asked the man whether he knew in which apartment Mrs. Tanner lived. The man replied that he was Mr. Tanner and that he was unaware that his wife had called the police. In the meanwhile, a neighbor appeared, complained that the noise in the upstairs apartment had disturbed her and wakened her children, and that she hoped that the police could keep this from occurring again. The officers asked Mr. Tanner to accompany them upstairs.

When the group reached the second floor, they were met outside the door of an apartment by Mrs. Tanner. On seeing her husband, she yelled, "What the hell are you doing here? I told you that I don't want you in my apartment again!" Officer Sheman replied, "Let's go in and talk this over."

The four went into the living room. A liquor bottle and an empty glass were apparent on a coffee table and the officers smelled liquor on Mrs. Tanner's breath. Questioning revealed that Mr. and Mrs. Tanner were separated. Their two children, for whom Mr. Tanner contributed twenty dollars a week for support, lived with Mrs. Tanner. Mrs. Tanner was a waitress. When she went to work in the mornings, she left her children, ages 4 and 2½, with her landlady.

Mrs. Tanner also informed the police officers that she refused her husband visitation privileges with the children at times and places other than those directed by the court. He was to have the children only on Saturdays, and he could not see them in her home. Mr. Tanner spoke up at this point. "I live in a furnished room. Where could I take the kids? I can't drive around with them in the car all day. And the baby is too young to go dragging around the city." Mrs. Tanner replied, "That's your problem.

If this arrangement doesn't satisfy you, my lawyer said the court will make arrangements so that you can see them there Saturday afternoons. But I don't want you in my apartment. Is that clear?" Turning to the officers, she said, "I put my children to bed at eight every night, and when do you think he shows up asking to see the kids? After nine. Does he think I'm going to wake the kids so that he can play with them at that hour?"

Officer Young interrupted Mrs. Tanner and said, "Well, ma'am, what can we do for you?" She explained, "The reason I called is because tonight he came knocking at the door after nine and asked to see the kids. I tried to slam the door in his face, but he forced his way into the apartment. We started arguing and then he began to punch me. He bit my arm so hard it was bleeding. I put this bandage on. He was wild—he started to punch me all over. I have marks all over my breasts and my sides."

HUDDLE QUESTIONS FOR "ARGUMENTATIVE MARRIED COUPLE"—"FACT FINDING"

Group A: What are some of the social and cultural factors which make for "success" or "failure" in marriage? Do all people view "happiness" or "success" in marriage the same way? How do the habits, attitudes and values which one has taken from his culture affect what one expects from marriage?

Group B: What are some of the behavioral and situational factors which make for "success" or "failure" in marriage? What constitutes a "successful" or "happy" marriage?

LEAD QUESTIONS FOR "ARGUMENTATIVE MARRIED COUPLE"—"FACT FINDING"

1. If you were Mr. Tanner, what sort of treatment would you have expected from the police? How do you think you would have felt under these circumstances?
2. Do you think the officers, although they said very little, took sides? Why is it inadvisable for a police officer to take sides?
3. If you were one of the police officers involved, would you

Discussion Points for "Argumentative Married Couple"—"Fact Finding"

Attitudes	Knowledges	Skills
How a person's "present mood" determines how he will react to others	The sense of value that people possess	Trying to pacify a person
Why officers take out their personal gripes on the public	The way certain people think	Answering coherent questions politely
	The civil rights laws	Explaining to people the ill effect their behavior has upon the community in which they reside
	Ethics and professionalism in police work	Determining the severity of a person's injury
	A person's point of view on a given issue	Making quick decisions on a course of action to follow
	The dynamics of personality	Taking actions that you think your supervisors would want you to take
		Getting all the facts from the people concerned at the scene of an incident
		Treating more educated people differently than less educated people

have investigated further to determine if Mrs. Tanner's story was true? How would you go about doing this?

4. Do you think the officers had sufficient information for making a decision? What additional facts would you want before you'd make any decisions?

5. Is it ethical for a police officer to offer advice? If you were to advise the couple on their behavior, how would you do it and what would you tell them?

CASE X—ARGUMENTATIVE MARRIED COUPLE
STAGE 2—DECISION MAKING

Group Material

Officer Sheman told Mrs. Tanner that a doctor should attend to her wounds. He asked her if there was someone that could come over to sit with the children while they took her to the hospital. Mrs. Tanner contacted her landlady who consented to come up and stay with the children.

While Mrs. Tanner was putting on her coat, she mentioned that she had sworn out a warrant for her husband's arrest. She showed the warrant receipt to the officers. The warrant, which was over one month old, had not yet been executed. She asked the police officers if it was still valid. Officer Young told her, "You can take this warrant receipt to a magistrate and he will take over from there."

After a short while, Officer Sheman said, "I think we're going to take you both down to the station and you can tell your story to the lieutenant." Mr. Tanner angrily stated, "Why are you pulling us in? You haven't even heard my story yet. Just because she's a woman doesn't mean she's right and I'm wrong." Officer Sheman then replied, "Well, we're going to take you in anyway and you can tell your story to the lieutenant down there. You have a perfect set-up here for a disorderly conduct charge, if nothing else."

HUDDLE QUESTIONS FOR "ARGUMENTATIVE MARRIED COUPLE"—"DECISION MAKING"

Group A: The role of women was once described as proper in

DISCUSSION POINTS FOR "ARGUMENTATIVE MARRIED COUPLE"—"DECISION MAKING"

Attitudes	Knowledges	Skills	Decisions
The reasons why couples argue	Why officers, should not take sides in a family dispute	Determining whether or not a person is telling the truth	To book or not to book someone
How a person's "present mood" determines how he will react to others	Why some people feel abused or "picked on" by the police	Taking into consideration the fact that some people are not aware that they violated the law before deciding upon what action to take toward them	That sufficient and legitimate cause for police action does or does not exist
	The way certain people think		To caution someone about his actions
	The senses of value that people possess		To offer advice
	A person's point of view on a given issue	Determining the severity of a person's injury	To ignore an offender's excuse for a misdemeanor
	The dynamics of human personality	Deciding whether or not a crime has been committed	To refuse a person's request
	The civil rights laws	Making a quick decision on a course of action to follow	

the church, the kitchen, and in child bearing. How correct is this point of view? Discuss and evaluate.

Group B: "The basic marital problem is that mutual neurotic dependence is mistaken for love." Discuss and evaluate.

LEAD QUESTIONS FOR "ARGUMENTATIVE ° MARRIED COUPLE"—"DECISION MAKING"

1. Why do you think the officers referred the case to the lieutenant? When should officers refer a case to someone else?
2. With whom do you think the officers were sympathizing? Were they justified or unjustified?
3. Do you think it's important for officers to take into consideration before taking action the fact that some people may not be aware that they violated the law? Under what circumstances should officers take this into consideration?
4. Why do you think the officers decided to take the Tanners to the station house? Would you have performed similarly? If not, what would you have done?
5. Do you think women receive preferential treatment from the police in general?

CASE X—ARGUMENTATIVE MARRIED COUPLE STAGE 3—COMSUMMATING THE PLAN

Group Material

The police lieutenant listened to the stories of both Mr. and Mrs. Tanner. Mrs. Tanner wept and begged the lieutenant to detain her husband "because he would come back and beat her again." She said that he was a "very spiteful person" and beat her even when they were living together.

The lieutenant complied with her request and told Mrs. Tanner that her husband would be held overnight on a disorderly conduct charge and that there would be a hearing on the following morning. The lieutenant also advised Mrs. Tanner to take her warrant receipt to a magistrate and to let him handle the matter for her.

DISCUSSION POINTS FOR "ARGUMENTIVE MARRIED COUPLE" — "CONSUMMATING THE PLAN"

Attitudes	*Knowledges*	*Skills*
How a person's "present mood" determines how he will react to others	Why some people may feel abused or "picked on" by the police	Arresting a belligerent spouse
Why officers take out their personal gripes on others	The way certain people think	Explaining to a married couple why their behavior is objectionable
	The sense of value that people possess	Explaining the constitutional rights to a citizen

HUDDLE QUESTIONS FOR "ARGUMENTATIVE MARRIED COUPLE"—"CONSUMMATING THE PLAN"

Group A: Were the police justified in arresting Mr. Tanner? Why? When should a belligerent person be arrested?

Group B: When a family breaks up, what is the effect on a child's: (1) need for affection, (2) feeling of security, (3) social opportunities, (4) need for physical necessities? How might these effects show in the child's behavior?

LEAD QUESTIONS FOR "ARGUMENTATIVE MARRIED COUPLE"—"CONSUMMATING THE PLAN"

1. Do you think that the role of the police officers should involve marriage counseling to the degree of helping married couples solve their disputes and differences?
2. What are some of the factors involved in "successful" parenthood?

SECTION III
LECTURE MATERIALS

LECTURE I

INDIVIDUAL AND GROUP SIMILARITIES AND DIFFERENCES

(30 minutes plus 30 minutes discussion)

Purpose: To demonstrate that more basic differences exist within an individual ethnic group than between ethnic groups.

U.S. is composed of people of diverse national origins (See Table 1)
Much lack of harmony

1. Restrictions against citizens of various foreign extractions
2. Often in contradiction with democracy race riots and violence occur

Accepted scientific facts
All men belong to a single species

1. Intra-fertile group with common genetic materials
2. Migration produced isolation

Inherent variability of genes
Genetic mutation and inbreeding has produced what we call "groups"
Continuous changes in people make any racial classification scheme transient

Basis for racial classification

1. *Skin color.* Strictly determined by carotene-melanin ratio together with pinkishness of blood vessels.

TABLE 1

NATIONAL ORIGIN OF FOREIGN BORN WHITE POPULATION OF PHILADELPHIA, 1950
(Source: Philadelphia Commission on Human Relations)

Country of Birth	Number
England	12,686
Scotland	6,311
Northern Ireland	693
Ireland (Eire)	24,203
Norway	736
Sweden	1,161
Denmark	512
Netherlands	288
France	1,872
Germany	19,736
Poland	20,281
Czechoslovakia	2,001
Austria	8,512
Yugoslavia	784
U. S. S. R.	53,906
Hungary	6,531
Lithuania	4,678
Finland	234
Rumania	3,679
Greece	2,061
Italy	48,721
Other Europe	3,119
Asia	2,984
Canada-French	372
Canada-Other	3,181
Mexico	268
Other America	1,473
All other and not reported	1,604

2. *Cephalic index.* Ratio of skull breadth to skull length; not supported by modern anthropology; fail when used alone to distinguish between Negroid, Caucasian, and Mongoloid groups; affected by dietary and climatic changes; same skull types found in widely separated races.

3. *Eye form.* Slant eyes found in white infants, Ethiopians, American Indians, and Mongoloid people.

4. *Eye color and hair texture.* Blues eyes and dark eyes found in all people; blond hair found in many people; wooly, wavy, or straight hair cannot be used alone for racial classification; Aus-

tralian Bushman has wavy hair like Caucasian, but is classified as Negroid.

5. *Nose shape.* "Jewish nose" found in entire East; straight American nose really a Roman nose.

6. *Height.* Varies with diet; Japanese born in this country are on the average taller than those born abroad; group averages usually 5 feet 5 inches, plus or minus 2 inches.

7. *Blood.* Four types, A, B, AB, and O, none of which (except O) can be intermixed, but all of which are found in all races; in transfusion, donor and recipient can have different racial backgrounds; thus, no blood type differences between groups.

8. *Sensory and psychological differences* between races

Primitive men possessed no greater sensory acuity than modern men; Woodworth's study of Eskimos, Patagonians, American Indians, Filipinos, etc.; differential training makes for apparent differences.

Behavioral development of Negro children faster than that of white; explainable on environmental basis; similarly, any measured differences in intelligence explainable on the same basis.

Klineberg's studies of effects of environment on intelligence as measured.

Any personality differences found are largely explainable on an environmental basis.

Value and attitude studies show similar values and attitudes between races when background is accounted for.

Self-attitude studies show racial awareness occurs early for whites and Negroes; Negroes less positive toward their race than whites.

Social perception studies show that attitudes of Negroes toward whites no more favorable than reverse.

TABLE 2
PHILADELPHIA HOME OWNERSHIP
(Source: Philadelphia Commission on Human Relations)

	1940 %	1950 %	1960 %
White			
Owner Occupied	43	62	68
Renter occupied	57	38	32
Non-White			
Owner occupied	10	30	43
Renter occupied	90	70	57

Family organization studies indicate greater family disorganization in Negro families as in general is the case in lower socio-economic groups.

Child rearing practice investigations indicate same differences exist between lower and middle class whites as between lower and middle class Negroes.

Birth control practices are highly correlated with urban birth, education, working mothers, etc., in both groups.

Demographic comparisons

Home ownership percentage a function of length of residing in city (see Table 2).

Whether or not home is classified by Census Bureau as "sound," "deteriorating" or "dilapidated" as much a function of owner *vs.* renter as a function of white *vs.* non-white (see Table 3).

TABLE 3
CONDITION IN 1959 OF PHILADELPHIA HOMES
(Source: Philadelphia Commission on Human Relations)

	White %	Non-White %
Owner occupied		
Sound	96	85
Deteriorating	4	14
Dilapidated	0	1
Renter occupied		
Sound	89	61
Deteriorating	10	31

TABLE 4

PHILADELPHIA EDUCATIONAL ATTAINMENT FOR WHITE AND NEGRO
GROUPS LIVING IN THE SAME NEIGHBORHOOD (1959)

(Source: Philadelphia Commission on Human Relations)

Schooling	Negro %	White %
Attended elementary school............	22.0	20.7
Graduated elementary school...........	19.0	19.0
Attended high school..................	29.0	29.4
Graduated high school.................	21.0	20.7
Attended college......................	5.0	5.5
Graduated college.....................	3.0	3.9
No schooling..........................	1.0	1.8

Educational attainment is almost the same for whites and Negroes when socio-economic status is equated (see Table 4).

Occupations of whites and Negroes are almost the same when area of residency (social status) is equated (see Table 5)

Conclusion: Few, if any, basic and lasting differences between races, aside from biological differences which are modifiable; any psychodynamic differences appear to be attributable to experience, culture, and training.

TABLE 5

PHILADELPHIA OCCUPATIONAL GROUPS FOR WHITE AND NEGRO GROUPS
LIVING IN THE SAME NEIGHBORHOOD (1959)

(Source: Philadelphia Commission on Human Relations)

Occupation	Negro %	White %
Professional or skilled.................	3.0	3.5
Manager or proprietor.................	9.0	9.5
Clerical..............................	8.0	9.5
Sales................................	1.0	1.2
Craftsman or skilled laborer...........	10.0	11.5
Domestic............................	7.0	5.2
Farm laborer........................	0.0	0.0
Farmer-Farm manager.................	0.0	0.0
Labor...............................	13.0	12.2
Operative/Service....................	24.0	22.3
Unemployed.........................	26.0	24.4

LECTURE II

PREJUDICE—ITS INSIDE THE INDIVIDUAL CAUSES

(30 minutes plus 30 minutes discussion)

Purpose: To point out and substantiate some of the intra-individual roots of prejudice.

A. Introduction

(Review of previous lecture). Last time we concluded that few, if any, lasting and non-modifiable differences exist among races and that any psychological differences which may exist can be explained on the basis of experience, culture, and training. Today, we explore some of the roots of racial prejudice.

What is racial prejudice? Racial prejudice refers to those attitudes or beliefs concerning any minority, racial, ethnic, or national group that are disadvantageous to the members of that group. The term, racial, is used in its popular and not scientific meaning. Hence, groups such as Negroes, Jews, Mexicans, Irish, etc., will be referred to as racial groups. These groups are considered as minority groups in this country because they differ from the dominant group in either their race, culture, or national origin.

B. Some causes of racial prejudice within a person

To understand why a person is racially prejudiced involves the understanding of the individual's needs, the demands that are satisfied by his negative beliefs and attitudes, and how racial prejudice serves the person in the solution of his personal problems.

Pathological personality systems. Not all racially

prejudiced people are mentally sick nor are all mentally sick people racially prejudiced, but the individual with a pathological personality sometimes manifests racially prejudiced attitudes in order to supports his deviant behavior.

1. Free-floating anxiety. Free-floating anxiety is based on the existence of tensions, having no reference to a particular or specific object. The tensions are reduced through attacks on others. Ultimately, an individual may learn to direct his aggressive behavior against a specific group.

   a. Paranoia. The paranoiac is usually a very suspicious person, a person suffering from delusions. A paranoiac may fix his suspicions on members of a minority group to justify his behavior.

2. Although the number of people whose overt prejudice is attributable to paranoia or free-floating anxiety is insignificant, these people nevertheless may exert a strong influence on others. Often these people are found as leaders of anti-racial mobs, organizations, and ideologies.

Frustration of various needs. Tensions arising out of the frustration of almost any significant need often find expression in aggressive acts which seem to allay temporarily the frustrated state. The targets of such aggression are not necessarily related to the frustrating situation.

1. This basis for racial prejudice is applicable to only a small segment of those who are racially prejudiced. Many people who are under great tension are not aggressive toward members of minority groups. There are a number of tension-reduction tech-

niques aside from hostility toward minority groups. Additionally, it is impossible to show that all people who are racially prejudiced have suffered more frustrations than people who are not racially prejudiced.

Rationalization of culturally disapproved behavior. Beliefs and attitudes of racial prejudice are developed in many racially prejudiced people in an attempt to resolve socially disapproved urges, such as impulses of cruelty, greed, and sexual aggression. A citizen must inhibit these urges because society disapproves of such behaviors.

1. The Southern politician who, striving for political eminence (a socially approved need), blocks the Negro from voting, rationalizes this behavior on the grounds that the Negro is mentally incapable of suffrage.

Repressed tensions. Tensions which are in conflict with one's moral ideology are often repressed. One possible effect of repressed tensions may be seen in projection (attributing to others one's personal shortcomings). When the projection is applied to a whole race of people, we have another example of racial prejudice. Franckel-Brunswick and Sanford found repressed hatred, meanness, jealousy, and suspicion toward parental figures among a group of girls who were determined anti-Semitics. The repressed tendencies and tensions find outlet in attitudes against certain racial groups which serve as scapegoats.

Self-regard and conformity. Many negative attitudes answer needs that are induced by the person's concept of his self; other negative attitudes serve to maintain the individual's identification with society.

1. Many beliefs and attitudes are organized to enhance one's feelings of self-esteem or

to remove a threat to such feelings. Many persons who have strong needs for superiority feelings may attempt to gratify these needs by finding other individuals or groups who can be subjugated to a "lower" class and to whom they can therefore feel superior.

2. An example of how racial prejudice may develop in an individual as an attempt to remove a threat to his feelings of pride and self-regard is found in the situation in which a person loses his job. Since he will not accept that he lost the job because he was an inferior worker, the person may explain his employer's action by claiming that the dismissal was the typical unscrupulous action of a Jew. Thus, in trying to save his pride and self-regard, the person develops attitudes of prejudice against Jews.

Need for group acceptance. Many people have needs for group acceptance. These needs may often be supported by negative attitudes, especially if the group with which the person wishes to identify is marked by such attitudes.

1. For example, a person may not be accepted into a particular country club, fraternity, or university faculty if his attitudes toward certain minority groups are not in accordance with those of the group he wishes to join. If it is important for him to become a member of a group which maintains negative attitudes, the individual, by conformity, adopts similar attitudes.

C. Conclusion

Thus, we see how racial prejudice can be used to justify a person's pathological aggressions, to rationalize culturally unacceptable needs, to rationalize culturally dis-

approved behaviors in order to satisfy culturally acceptable aspirations, to reduce repressed tensions, to develop
feelings of self-regard, to protect oneself against threats
to such feelings, and to become accepted by certain
groups. There is no single reason by which we can explain all racial or religious prejudice.

LECTURE III

PREJUDICE—ITS OUTSIDE THE INDIVIDUAL CAUSES

(30 minutes plus 30 minutes discussion)

Purpose: To point out and substantiate some of the extra-individual roots of prejudice.

A. Introduction

(Review of previous lecture). The previous discussion described some of the intra-individual roots of negative intergroup attitudes. These involved an understanding of: (1) within individual needs and demands, (2) tensions within the person, (3) the desire for social approval, and (4) individual maintenance of self-regard. The discussion today focuses on some of the environmental or outside the individual sources of prejudice.

B. Definitions

Ethnic group. A group of people who have in common one or more of the following: religion, racial origin, national origin, or language and cultural traditions.

In the U.S., most individuals are members of several ethnic groups. The most important group for a particular individual depends partly on his attitudes and partly on the attitudes of other people.

Ethnic attitude. A tendency to react in specific ways to another individual or group of individuals (e.g., having favorable or unfavorable beliefs about other individuals or groups, and friendly or unfriendly feelings toward them).

Prejudice. An ethnic attitude in which the reactions to other individuals and groups are negative.

C. Some of the extra-individual roots of negative intergroup attitudes and behaviors

How and when? Social scientists are agreed that ethnic attitudes are learned and not inherited.

> Goodman's investigation of Negro and white nursery school children (who all lived in or near mixed neighorhoods) shows a relationship between racial awareness and age. High awareness did not appear before age 4, and low awareness did not persist beyond age 5.
>
> Zeligs found that by age 11 children's attitudes toward various ethnic groups have become fairly well stabilized in that their order of preference for different ethnic groups is relatively the same as it is for adults.
>
> Minard's study with high school students showed a steady increase in prejudice from the seventh through the twelfth grades.
>
> Criswell's study on racial behavior in grade school children led to the conclusion that at first the child selects playmates and school chums on the strength of an individual "test," personal experience, and pleasant or unpleasant situations. As the child grows older, his attention to or repulsion from members of a given group is dependent upon previously acquired attitudes toward that group.

Economic competition

> Economic competition is frequently a source for the development of negative intergroup attitudes. It is often those people who feel economically threatened by a particular group that exhibit prejudiced attitudes.

1. As a result of the fear of economic competition this country has enforced certain restrictions on immigration.
2. Certain unions restrict membership to majority groups.

Learning racial prejudice. How does teaching, training, guidance, and propaganda, induce and spread attitudes of racial prejudice?

Learning plays a significant role in the development of beliefs and attitudes.

1. *Direct training.* Among some groups of whites, the child is taught to regard the Negro in a derogatory fashion. He is told that the Negro is dirty and breeds disease. The child is often punished if he is caught playing with a Negro child. Equally potent and effective is the propaganda emanating from prejudiced organizations.
2. *Indirect training.* Indirect training occurs in situations in which a person overhears derogatory comments issued against some particular individual or group of people, e.g., "Jim, the porter, uses all his money to get drunk—like all colored people," or anecdotes and jokes told about Negroes. Racially prejudiced beliefs and attitudes are thus formed and supported.
3. *Supports in the fictitious world.* Columbia University's Bureau of Applied Social Research performed a study of the characters of magazine short stories. This study provides us with another instance of how our environment indirectly teaches racial prejudice. In the stories analyzed, most of the identifiable acceptable characters were Anglo-Saxon. Racketeers, thieves, gam-

blers, and other non-sympathetic characters were seldom Anglo-Saxon. There seems to be less racial stereotypy in the various forms of entertainment (stage, movies, radio, TV) but heroes and heroines still tend to be white, Protestant, Anglo-Saxons.

D. Conclusion

Negative intergroup attitudes can stem from environmental roots as well as on a within individual basis. Typical environmental roots are:

Learning from parents
Economic competition
Status mobility and maintenance
Learning from teachers
Indirect training
Supports in the fictitious world

LECTURE IV

HOW AN INDIVIDUAL SUPPORTS HIS ATTITUDES

(30 minutes plus 30 minutes discussion)

Purpose: To yield an understanding of how an individual distorts reality in order to support his negative intergroup attitudes.

A. Introduction

(Review of previous lecture). To this point we have seen how negative intergroup attitudes may be developed. These were ascribed to sources within the individual such as need and value systems, justification of pathological aggressive tendencies, rationalization of socially disapproved needs, as well as to extra—individual sources such as learning from parents, economic competition, status mobility and maintenance, learning from teachers, indirect training, and supports in the fictitious world. Today we will discuss how an individual may artificially find support in the environment for his prejudices.

B. (First perform a demonstration illustrating the effects of needs or prior experience on perception)

C. Functional selectivity

Our perceptions (what we see) are often influenced by our beliefs, social ideals, morals, previous learning, and cultural frames of reference. An example of how our perceptions are influenced by our culture is that of an American tourist and a Mexican at a bullfight. The American might perceive and stress the pain to the animal and the messiness of the scene whereas the Mexican might perceive and stress the skill of the performer and the fine technical points involved.

D. Examples of stereotyping or biased perception of various groups

> All Negroes are dirty
> All Jews are shrewd
> All Italians are quick tempered

Because many Americans ascribe certain traits to various groups, their perceptions of individual members of the groups may be distorted as a result of these biases. Thus, because of the stereotyped notion that Negroes are unintelligent, any and all Negroes are regarded as unintelligent.

Kernel of truth

> Klineberg coined the term "kernel of truth" which he applied to stereotypes. There may be some objective reality in a stereotype when it is applied to certain members of a minority group. This objective reality may exist only to a small or insignificant degree. The prejudiced person seizes this reality, exaggerates it, and applies it to all members of the group.

Cues in stereotypy

> *Physical cues.* Physical signs are characteristic of ethnic groupings even though these signs may not apply to all members of the group. The racially prejudiced person who is aware of certain differentiating physical characteristics has an induced need or mental set that requires him to be able to recognize a member of the group against which he is prejudiced. Allport and Kramer's experiment shows that the prejudiced person will maximize perceptual cues and these cues will be detected more often by

the prejudiced person than by the non-prejudiced person. (Demonstration here).

Psychological cues. It is often assumed by the prejudiced person that psychological traits distinguish various ethnic groupings. Consider clannish behavior. Many prejudiced persons ascribe this trait to members of minority groups. This may be a genuine trait which can be frequently observed. However, racial prejudice, in itself, affects the personality of the victim and if members of minority groups are not accepted by other groups, then they seek to satisfy the need for belongingness within their own group.

Social cues. Occupations, schools, places of residence, and church membership may constitute social cues which serve as environmental supports for racial prejudice. Thus, one group may be perceived as properly being laundrymen, another as shoeshine boys, and so on. Labor unions have been guilty, at one time or another, of practicing segregation among their members or of discriminating against certain racial groups.

Summary. Of the three types of cues in stereotyping, physical, psychological, and social, that reinforce prejudice, the social cues are the most important. The reasons for this are: (a) they provide the clearest cues for perception, (b) the social stigma is forced on certain ethnic groups by civil law, religious policy, business practices, etc.

Stereotypy's faults

It does not allow for individual differences which are greater within groups than between groups.

It overlooks environmental pressures which lead members of a particular group to develop certain traits which are commonly ascribed to the entire group.

It overlooks experiences which contradict the generalization made in stereotyped thinking.

As long as we organize people into groups and ascribe certain traits to the groups, our perception of specific individuals will be distorted and influenced by our perception of the group. Although it is difficult to avoid organizing people into groups, there is no reason why groupings must be based on skin color, religion, or nationality.

E. Conclusion

Once a person has developed his negative intergroup attitudes he seizes certain physical, psychological, and social cues to reinforce and sustain his bias.

LECTURE V

PERSONALITY AND BEHAVIOR

(30 minutes plus 30 minutes discussion)

Purpose: To develop in police officers an appreciation and understanding of the behaviors, attitudes, and motives or reasons why individuals act in certain ways.

A. Introduction

Previous lectures have pointed out that negative attitudes often find their roots in the environment and/or on a within individual basis. Once developed, these attitudes are sustained through various cues. This lecture shows some of the further basis for behavioral development in relationship to intergroup situations or social behavior.

B. Effect of blocked biological drives on social behavior

It is through various techniques that the individual tries to overcome the frustration caused by the deprivation of a basic biological need such as food, water or sexual deprivation.

Self-assertion. When his biological drives were blocked, the individual may have learned that to be self-assertive (that is, to press and demand to achieve one's goals) is a successful method of satisfying some biological goal (food, water, sex).

C. Similar mechanisms may also apply in social drives

As an example of how self-assertion may operate in a frustrating situation, think of the child whose self-assertive and offensive behaviors are suppressed by his parents. In an effort to overcome the frustration which results because he cannot continue to react to a certain situation in a self-assertive manner, the individual has several alternatives to which he may resort.

He can identify with his parents and do the sort of thing which they and others approve. Thus, he will direct his self-assertion into a socially approved method of attacking his problem, i.e., he will conform to group norms.

The child may learn that by being self-abasive (that is, by being extremely submissive and yielding to the wishes of others) he will reduce the amount of his punishment. Self-abasement is accompanied by repression. The child will repress the resultant hostility against his parents. The repressed hostilities tend to come out later in a variety of indirect ways—self-punishment, crime, radicalism, aggression against inferiors, negative intergroup attitudes, etc.

Reaction formation. Tensions often accompany repressed hostilities which seek relief through a variety of different defense mechanisms or tension relievers. One such tension reliever is called reaction formation. That is, repressed aggressions may express themselves in behavioral patterns that are the reverse sort of behavior. Thus, instead of being aggressive, the individual may become very submissive and sympathetic. A pacifist may have been driven over to his philosophies as a result of repressed hostilities and now they are expressed in the individual's oversolicitousness, kindness, and non-aggressive tendencies.

Introjection. Another tension reliever which may operate to relieve repressed hostilities is introjection. For example, hostility against one's parents may be converted into hostility against oneself. The child will, under these circumstances, resort to punishing himself. Suicides, neurotic invalidism, alcoholism, and many types of accidents often turn out to be expressions of an unconscious need for self-punishment.

Symbolization. The process of symbolization is another tension reliever. Repressed hostility may express itself in hostility against some symbolic substitute of the frustrating agent (against the parents, in the case of the child). Two typical expressions of this hostility are seen in crime and radicalism.

> Alexander and Healy performed psychoanalytical studies on 20 male criminals. They showed that a large amount of the criminal behavior was an expression of an unconscious desire to get even with society, where society was the symbolic substitute for the parents. These criminals thought of their parents as having been cruel and unfair.

> Police officers who exhibit excessive brutality may also be exhibiting this process.

> Radicalism is often an outshoot of or a protest against cruelties or injustices to which an individual may feel he was subjected at some time in his life. Thus, we might find radicalism in certain Negroes who are impatient for legal enforcement of civil rights laws.

Displacement. Tension resulting from repression may take the form of hostility or aggression against "inferiors." We often see this mechanism in operation when a child releases his hostilities against a younger sibling after the older child has been admonished or punished by his parents. This mechanism is also characteristic of the relations between poor whites and Negroes (the poor whites "take it" from their superiors and in turn "dish it out" to their "inferiors" or Negroes).

Projection. Repressed hostilities against a parent or superior may find expression through the mechanisms of identification with the group and projection. In this instance, hostilities are directed toward those who are

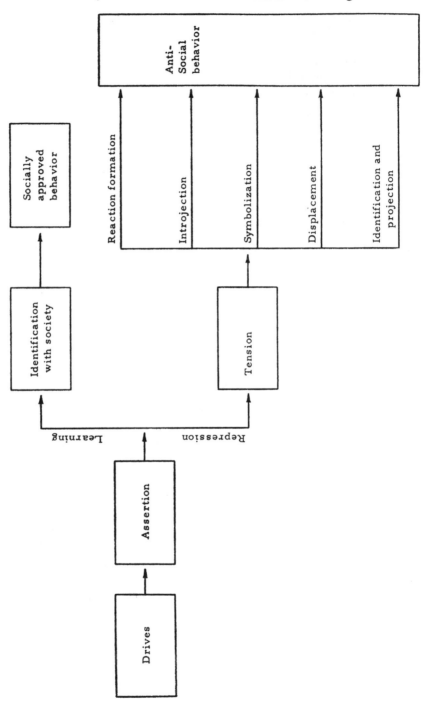

not members of the group, along with the accompanying feeling (due to projection) that it is the outsiders who are really guilty.

D. Conclusion

When drives are blocked people resort to various unconscious mechanisms as a method for expressing these drives. In intergroup and other situations, these may take the form of:

Reaction formation
Introjection
Symbolization
Displacement
Group identification and projection

LECTURE VI

CONTROLLING RACIAL PREJUDICE

(3v minutes plus 30 minutes discussion)

Purpose: To demonstrate principles and programs designed to develop an acceptance of integrated situations.

A. Introduction

A number of the lectures of this series have pointed out the nature of prejudice, its causes, and how it is sustained. This lecture attempts to show some of the techniques available for controlling prejudice.

B. Elimination of the motivational roots of prejudice

Eliminate those need structures which are prejudice prone.

The positive approach. Reduce frustrations by satisfaction of man's common and socially acceptable needs in the economic, social technological, and political policy areas.

1. Mintz found evidence that when the economic level of the South drops, the number of lynchings tends to rise.

2. Establish and maintain adequate minimum wage laws; abolish poll taxes; maintain cultural, fraternal and recreational organizations which provide self-expressive opportunities in leadership, and expression of esthetic, cultural, and recreational needs.

The therapeutic approach. Create emotional security and maturity and remove the effects of past traumatic emotional experiences.

1. Therapeutically oriented programs should consider psychological security from infancy, parent-child relationships, group behavior, and the indoctrination of approved ideologies, morals, and ethics.

    a. Psychologically oriented centers have proven their value in decreasing faulty beliefs and negative attitudes in solving emotional problems and modifying emotional attitudes.

    b. Group therapeutic sessions provide good orientation for those who need to gain social experience from relationships outside the family, or for those who need to learn how to get along with others through the adjustment of certain personality traits.

    c. Clinics for parent training and vocational, industrial, educational, marriage, and child guidance can provide direct attacks on prejudice.

C. Perceptual aspects of racial prejudice

   Remove physical, psychological, and social environmental supports that allow people to perceive members of minority groups as having unique characteristics which other people do not have.

   Changing the objective qualities of members of minority groups.

    1. The grouping of people perceptually does not create racial prejudice; however, it helps to foster certain beliefs and attitudes. These attitudes may be favorable as well as unfavorable.

        a. *Acculturate.* Acculturation involves the elimination of certain social cues that might set certain groups apart, e.g., names, food habits, and recreational patterns. However, there are objections to acculturation in that the American way of life might not be as rich and colorful if certain distinctive patterns of food, dress, speech, literature, music, and games were abandoned. The psychological objections to acculturation are that, for many members of minority groups, these provide strong feelings of pride and self respect. Through acculturation a loss of morale (e.g., the Lewin study) might occur. This could lead to maladjustment and consequently to an increase in intergroup tensions or in new psychological mechanisms such as aggressiveness or assertiveness. These side effects will vary in intensity for different individuals, for not all members of minority groups possess strong feelings of belongingness to their group. Hence, many people will gain emotional security by conformity with the majority group. In determining the value of this type of program, we should consider the dangers of the side effects that may occur and weigh these against the long term effects of the program.

b. *Improve the services available to members of minority groups.* Such services are involved with education (i.e., remove the stigma of the uneducated Negro), nutrition, medicine, and recreation.

c. *Eliminate segregation through legal, religious, and economic practices.* Such programs meet with much resistance and there are many barriers to abolishing segregation, but it is the most significant of the programs discussed. Minority group members, themselves, may object to eliminating segregation (e.g., the Frazier study) for various reasons, e.g., Negro physicians may advocate separate hospitals for the added opportunities they will have in developing their skills and serving their "own people." Several studies have been performed which demonstrate the favorable effects of integration. Examples are the Northrup study of the Machinist's Union and the Curran study of the National Maritime Union. Segregational practices were abolished, and through educational programs, racial beliefs and attitudes of many of its members were changed. The Brophy study of members of the same union showed correlations revealing that through more contact with Negroes, white sailors became less prejudiced.

d. *Change reporting practices of newspapers and media* which support certain beliefs and attitudes of racial prejudice, e.g., identifying a criminal as Negro but not doing so when the criminal is white or protestant.

e. *Change the portrayal of racial characteristics* in fiction and advertising, i.e., preventing the consistent portrayal of minority group members as being undesirable.

D. Educational aspects of racial prejudice

Manipulating the person's environment in order to change his motivational structure and perceptions

Education through the schools

1. *Use appropriate textbooks.* Books that present the problems of the adjustment of minority group children and teach democracy will have beneficial effects on the elimination of prejudice. These books should not stress the differences among various groups.

2. *Establish the proper social atmosphere in the schools.* Teachers themselves must not be racially prejudiced and the school must not be segregated for pupils as well as for teachers.

3. *Obtain support from the parents through adult education courses.* Without the support of the parents, the school program cannot succeed (Chatto and Halligan's Springfield plan).

4. *Provide intercultural courses which stress intercultural relations.* Students should be taught to appreciate the contributions made by the people of different racial and ethnic groups, and students should be made to realize the value and importance of cooperation among all people (Fisk's study on good and bad intercultural programs).

5. *Teaching democratic behaviors and skills.* These would involve such behaviors as working and cooperating with children of different racial groups and backgrounds.

Education through adult interracial community programs. These programs often result in significantly decreasing racial prejudice. It is important that people of different racial backgrounds not be perceived in the context of a member of a minority but as a member of the community working with other community members on local problems and programs.

Education through mass publicity programs. However, the Lazarsfeld and Merton study pointed out that radio and film propaganda often reach the people who are in the least need for such messages (more members of the group who are being discussed listen to these messages than do members to whom the messages are being directed). The disadvantages of education through the mass media are that they reinforce the democratic beliefs of many but do not come across to many people whose attitudes and beliefs are being challenged.

E. Conclusion

Prejudice is controlled by attacking its

Motivational roots
Social supports
Perceptual aspects
Educational roots

No one measure can work effectively in all cases.

LECTURE VII

MYTHS AND FACTS REGARDING THE BACKGROUND FOR CRIME

(30 minutes plus 30 minutes discussion)

Purpose: To replace certain popular misconceptions about crime and its background with facts and to provide an understanding of why certain people may act as they do.

A. Among the most popular misconceptions is the myth that immigrants to the United States commit a disproportionate percentage of the crime.

Historically, each successive migrational wave has been blamed for high crime rates.

In 1830, it was said about the Irish: "As long as we are overwhelmed with Irish immigrants . . . thefts, incendiaries, murders which prevail, all arise from this source."*

In 1850, it was written about the Irish and Germans that: "We must, as a people, act upon this foreign element, or it will act upon us. Like the vast Atlantic, we must decompose and cleanse the impurities which rush into our midst, or, like the inland lake, we will receive the poison in our whole national system."**

Today, the same is said about current in-migrant groups such as the Puerto Ricans. Oddly enough,

---

* Barach, Dorothy (editor): *Letters of John Pinard.* New York, New York Historical Society, 1941.

** *Report of the Select Committee appointed to examine into conditions of tenement houses in New York and Brooklyn.* New York State Assembly Document No. 205, 1857.

such accusations are made by immigrants themselves or by their first generation decendants.

Studies comparing the crime rates of immigrants with native born Americans do not support this point of view. In fact, in proportion to their number, native born Americans commit more crimes than those who are foreign born.

Table 1 is a abstract of comparative crime rates for the year 1942 of native born and foreign born residents.

TABLE 1

OFFENSES BY NATIVITY FOR 1942*

	Born in U. S. A. %	Foreign Born %
Charge		
Larceny	17.5	7.4
Burglary	15.3	4.4
Car theft	8.9	1.5
Robbery	8.1	3.7
Rape	4.0	3.3
Manslaughter	1.8	1.8
Murder	2.1	1.9

* Abstracted from Gray J.: *Psychology in Human Affairs.* New York. McGraw-Hill, 1946.

It is true that the foreign born are higher in some categories of crime, such as violation of liquor and drug laws, and that certain foreign born age groups commit a disproportionate share of the crime. Much of this can be ascribed to ignorance of the laws, or dissatisfaction with social and economic opportunity.

More recent studies also supported this conclusion of a depressed crime rate among in-migrants.

1. Sutherland found that the arrest and imprisonment rate is about twice as high for native born in comparison with foreign born.

Reasons for lowers crime rate among in-migrants are:

High sensitivity to their popular image
Better institutions of control and primary relationships
An appreciation of the advantages of democracy

B. Another popular conception is that an identifiable "criminal type" exists.

Any descriptive factor such as age, sex, race, or marital conditions may be important in one criminal act and not in another.

Age. Age is related to the type of crime that people commit but not the number of crimes. Thus, younger persons tend to commit crimes of violence, while older people get involved with embezzlement and frauds. Drunkenness, disorderly conduct, and petty larceny are found at all ages.

Mental characteristics

1. The crime rate for feeble-minded is not greater than for normals (we should remember that feeble-minded are not bad, only highly suggestible.)
2. Convicts when tested by Murchison on an intelligence examination received higher scores than did white soldiers.

Sex. Men commit more crimes than women, but when women do commit crimes, it is usually of a highly emotional, motivated nature. Offenses ranking higher for women than for men include murder, manslaughter, aggravated assault, receiving stolen property, and commercialized vice. Men are higher on robbery, burglary, auto theft, and embezzlement.

1. There is no evidence that female crime is different in emphasis because of genetic or biological reasons. It is believed that the

difference obtained is a function of the cultural role placed by society on women.

Personality. While it is not possible to include a complete study of all personality dysfunctions and their causes, it can be said that many personality "types" are susceptible to chronic alcoholism, prostitution, homosexuality, and the like. Moreover, there is little or no evidence for a biological basis for these. Most current thinkers ascribe these illnesses to tensions related to socio-cultural phenomena.

1. Many psychopaths never come into contact with the law. They are more "odd" than criminal. Other psychopaths break laws.

In a study of 10,000 criminals in New York State, only 8% were classified as either neurotics or psychotics.

Other examples of people with sound personalities who have committed crimes:

1. TV quiz shows
2. Petty thievery of clerks in chain stores
3. Petty thievery of clientele in restaurants
4. Thievery of hotel linens

C. Conclusion

Simple explanations for the cause of crime are not acceptable. Usually a variety of factors related to complex and interactive social and cultural factors can be related to crime in a causal way.

LECTURE VIII

COMMUNITY HUMAN RELATIONS RESOURCES

(30 minutes plus 30 minutes discussion)

Purpose: To develop in police officers a recognition and awareness of the role of associated community human relations agencies.

A. Introduction

There are a number of national and local intergroup community relations agencies functioning. These agencies are staffed by professional people who devote themselves to defending and extending basic and inalienable rights, as defined in our Constitution, to all citizens of this country.

B. Of the many agencies existing, only a few will be discussed. This does not mean that those agencies not emphasized in this discussion are of lesser importance or effectiveness. Our purpose is to demonstrate the scope of the available resources, the broadness of general interest in the problems discussed throughout these meetings, and the importance of cooperating with these agencies in their on-going work.

These agencies are generally anxious to cooperate with the police and can constitute an important aid to the police officer in his day to day work.

National Association for the Advancement of Colored People

Purpose is to secure for Negroes the same privileges and rights that are granted to other citizens throughout the country.

[156]

Supported by its members, who belong to all races, religions, and come from various national origins.

Services are extended in many areas in order to secure for Negroes the equalities of freedom that white people enjoy:

1. Education
2. Employment
3. Housing

American Civil Liberties Union

Purpose is to extend the rights and liberties as guaranteed by the Bill of Rights of the United States Constitution to all citizens regardless of race, creed, religion, or national origin.

Services are focused on work in courts, legislative bodies, executive agencies, and in the field of public opinion.

1. Freedom of speech
2. Freedom of assembly
3. Religious freedom
4. The right to due process
   a. Freedom from unreasonable searches and seizures
5. Equal treatment under law for everyone

National Conference of Christians and Jews

Purpose is to promote understanding among people of all religions and racial groups.

Like the others, it is supported through the voluntary subscriptions of its members.

Educational programs are emphasized to:

1. Equip people to live together in harmony despite religious and racial differences
2. Equip people to respect the religious beliefs of others

The NCCJ seeks to guard against religious indifference and supports intergroup relationships without compromising religious beliefs.

Other active agencies include:

American Friends Service Committee
American Jewish Committee
American Jewish Congress
Anti-Defamation League of B'nai B'rith
Jewish Community Relations Council
Jewish Labor Committee
Race Relations Committee of the Society of Friends

1. Each of these possesses a specific function and goal in the network of agencies which serve to promote harmonious intergroup relationships, equality of opportunity, and guarantee of Constitutional rights for all persons.

C. Conclusion

A number of intergroup agencies exist. Each of these agencies possesses a somewhat unique purpose within the common goal of harmonious intergroup relations and equality of opportunity. Through cooperation with these agencies in their attempts to reach these socially acceptable goals, the police officer can make an important contribution to the social structure.

LECTURE IX

CIVIL RIGHTS AND PROFESSIONALISM IN POLICE WORK

(30 minutes plus 30 minutes discussion)

Purpose: To reemphasize, in the mind of the individual officer, the civil rights guaranteed to all citizens by the Constitution and to point out certain professional trends in police work.

A. Civil Rights

Police derive their power from:
Constitution of the U.S.
Federal laws and court decisions
State laws
Municipal laws and ordinances

One of police powers given by law is that of arrest.

The general rule is that the amount of force used in making an arrest must not be more than is necessary for self-protection.

The use of deadly force is to be frowned upon, especially if the offender is a misdemeanant.

Search and seizure

The Fourth Amendment protects all citizens from unreasonable search.

For a search to be reasonable, it must:
1. Be made by warrant
2. Be incident to lawful arrest
3. Be made when there are reasonable grounds

[159]

for believing that evidence of a crime will be uncovered

A search is unreasonable if:

1. It is exploratory in nature
2. It goes beyond the authorization of the warrant

Of course, an arrested person may be searched for weapons and for evidence; this search may be extended without a warrant to his car or to the room in which he was arrested.

The Fourteenth Amendment

Contains the "due process" clause; it follows from this that a coerced confession is not admissible legal evidence.

The First Amendment

Guarantees the rights of free speech, the right to religious choice, and the right to peaceable assembly.

1. A "clear and present danger" must exist before an assembled crowd can be broken up.

The question is whether effective police practice can take place without some infringement on these rights. The answer to this question is probably "No." However as we "trade-off" some of these rights in the name of effective police practice, we give away some of our freedoms. The extent that each citizen (including police officers) wishes to do this will vary from individual to individual, depending upon which he feels is the more paramount. It is also pointed out that when a police officer deprives a citizen of certain of his rights, the police officer is loosening the strength of his own constitutional guarantees.

B. Public relations aspects of police work

The work of the police is little understood by the public who often view the police officer as a "cop" from the Keystone comedy or "ignorant grafter" point of view. These stereotypes and attitudes in the citizens develop in the same way as do the other unhealthy attitudes and prejudices discussed in this series.

Thus, while the public demands better police work, prejudice, pride, stereotypes, reports of brutality, motion pictures, etc., have built up a picture which is hard to erase.

Just as corporations are conscious of their public image, so are all responsible police officers.

To help erase this picture, it is the responsibility of every officer to act in a professional manner. Professionalism for police officers as for all other professions includes:

Constant training
  1. Reading of books and professional journals
  2. Participation in community activities
  3. Home study

Adherence to a code of ethics
  1. Fairness to all people
  2. Non-brutality
  3. Courtesy and altruism
  4. Adherence to conduct norms
  5. Adherence to moral norms
  6. Professional manner

Consciousness that any individual act may reflect either positively or negatively on the image of the police

Day to day behavior of police officers should always be such as to improve the public image of the police.